ST. SERAPHIM OF SAROV

Тропа́рь, гла́съ д҃:

Ю́ности хрⷭ҇та̀ возлюби́лъ є҆сѝ, бл҃же́нне, и҆ томꙋ̀ є҆ди́ному рабо́тати пла́меннѣ вожделѣ́въ, непреста́нною моли́твою и҆ трꙋдо́мъ въ пꙋсты́ни подвиза́лсѧ є҆сѝ, ᲂу҆ми́леннымъ же се́рдцемъ любо́вь хрⷭ҇то́вꙋ стѧжа́въ, и҆збра́нникъ возлю́бленъ бж҃їѧ мт҃ре ꙗ҆ви́лсѧ є҆сѝ. сегѡ̀ ра́ди вопїе́мъ тѝ: спаса́й на́съ мл҃твами твои́ми, серафі́ме, прпⷣбне ѻ҆́тче на́шъ.

Конда́къ, гла́съ в҃:

Мі́ра красотꙋ̀ и҆ ꙗ҆́же въ не́мъ тлѣ̑ннаѧ ѡ҆ста́вивъ, прпⷣбне, въ саро́вскꙋю ѡ҆би́тель всели́лсѧ є҆сѝ: и҆ та́мѡ а҆́гг҃льски пожи́въ, мнѡ́гимъ пꙋ́ть бы́лъ є҆сѝ ко спⷭ҇е́нїю: сегѡ̀ ра́ди и҆ хрⷭ҇то́съ тебѐ, ѻ҆́тче серафі́ме, просла́ви, и҆ да́ромъ и҆сцѣле́нїй и҆ чꙋде́съ ѡ҆богатѝ. тѣ́мже вопїе́мъ тѝ: ра́дꙋйсѧ, серафі́ме, прпⷣбне ѻ҆́тче на́шъ.

Apolytikion. Mode IV.

Thou didst love Christ from thy youth, O blessed one, and ardently desiring to work for Him alone, thou didst struggle in the wilderness with constant prayer and labour; and having acquired love for Christ with compunction of heart, thou didst prove to be the beloved favorite of the Mother of God. Wherefore, we cry to thee: Save us by thy prayers, O Seraphim, our righteous Father.

Kontakion. Mode II.

Having left the beauty of the world and what is corrupt therein, O Saint, thou didst settle in Sarov Monastery. And having lived there an angelic life, thou wast for many the way unto salvation. Wherefore, Christ hath glorified thee, O Father Seraphim, and hath enriched thee with the gift of healing and miracles. Therefore we cry to thee: Rejoice, O Seraphim, our righteous Father.

St. Seraphim of Sarov

MODERN ORTHODOX SAINTS

5

ST. SERAPHIM OF SAROV

Widely beloved Mystic, Healer, Comforter, and Spiritual Guide. An account of his Life, Character and Message, together with a very edifying Conversation with his disciple Motovilov on the acquisition of the Grace of the Holy Spirit, and the Saint's Spiritual Counsels.

By

CONSTANTINE CAVARNOS

and

MARY-BARBARA ZELDIN

INSTITUTE FOR BYZANTINE
AND MODERN GREEK STUDIES
115 Gilbert Road
Belmont, Massachusetts 02178
U.S.A.

92
Se 65
8106161(

PREFACE

In the other volumes of this series that have already appeared in print, saints have been presented about whom little or nothing was available in any language other than the Greek. Those volumes came to fill obvious gaps in the English language literature that pertains to Eastern Orthodox spirituality. The preparation of the present volume was prompted by other considerations. A number of publications on St. Seraphim of Sarov are available in English. Some of these are accounts of his life; others offer part of his teaching, particularly that contained in *A Conversation with the Saint* by N. A. Motovilov. These publications are undoubtedly useful. However, a study of them shows the need of a book that is more comprehensive than any of them, one that offers at once a detailed account of St. Seraphim's life and teaching, and in addition a substantial introduction to both, placing them in the context of the long tradition of Orthodox monastic spirituality. The present volume is intended to meet this need.

The long Introductory chapter sums up the main facts about the life, character and conduct of St. Seraphim, and amply discusses his place in the Orthodox monastic tradition. It seeks to correct the tendency in recent years of presenting him as a kind of oddity — an oddity standing outside this tradition and inaugurating another form of spirituality, one supposedly superior to the traditional Orthodox. By means of many references to the long tradition of Orthodox monasticism, it shows that St. Seraphim remained faithful to this tradition, never deviating from it.

The beautiful life of St. Seraphim that follows the Introductory was written specially for this volume by a scholar who has a wide acquaintance with Russian history and culture: Dr. Mary-Barbara Zeldin, Professor of Philosophy and Religion at Hollins College, Virginia. She also provided the fresh translations of the remarkable *Conversation* and the *Spiritual Counsels* of the Saint that come next. Her contributions are a fruit of long and painstaking scholarly research and deep appreciation of the importance of the life, character and message of St. Seraphim. Like my Introductory, they appear in print for the first time.

Thanks are due to Dr. John Johnstone, Jr., for reading this book in manuscript and suggesting various improvements, and to Holy Transfiguration Monastery at Brookline, Massachusetts, for providing the translations of the Apolytikion and the Kontakion of St. Seraphim, as well as the photograph for the frontispiece. The photograph is of a contemporary icon of the Saint in the monastery's possession.

May, 1980   CONSTANTINE CAVARNOS

viii

ACKNOWLEDGEMENTS

Most of the original material and of the first publications concerning St. Seraphim was lost or became unavailable after the Russian Bolshevik Revolution of 1917 and the subsequent Civil War. In obtaining sources for the "Life" and for my selections from the "Conversation with the Saint" and the "Spiritual Counsels," I was assisted by many interested friends and colleagues, who directed me to sources or provided me with them, sometimes even from their personal libraries. In this connection, I wish particularly to thank Rt. Rev. Fr. Fyodor Kovalchuk of Youngstown, Ohio, Professor Nicholas Zernov of Oxford University, Rev. Fr. John Meyendorff of St. Vladimir's Seminary, Professor Pierre Pascal of the University of Paris, David Chavchavadze and Mrs. Nina Bouroff, both of Washington, D.C. I am also indebted to Mrs. Natalia Heseltine of Geneva, Rev. Fr. Nicholas Bacalis of Roanoke, Virginia, and Rev. Alvord Beardslee of Hollins College for their assistance with translations and their editorial advice on the manuscript. I wish also to thank Professor Charles Morlang of Hollins College and Mr. Rupert Barneby of the New York Botanical Gardens for their interest and thoroughness in identifying the plant aegopod. In addition, I wish to thank the Holy Trinity Monastery in Jordanville, N. Y., the University of Virginia Library, and the Slavic and East European Division of the University of Illinois Library, particularly Mr. Harold Leich, for their invaluable assistance. Finally, I wish to thank Hollins College for its several grants which defrayed a part of the expenses of my research, and Mrs. Lois Zook and Mrs. Elizabeth Dungan for their typing of my manuscript.

MARY-BARBARA ZELDIN

Hollins College

CONTENTS

INTRODUCTORY

By Constantine Cavarnos

I

The blessed Seraphim, who is one of the most popular modern Orthodox saints, was born on July 19, 1759, in the town of Kursk, about 300 miles south of Moscow. The son of Isidore and Agatha Moshnin, he was named Prokhor at Holy Baptism. In 1762, his father died, and the whole responsibility of bringing up Prokhor was assumed by his mother.

At the age of seven, Prokhor fell from a high scaffolding of a church which his father had undertaken to build and whose construction was completed by his mother after Isidore's death. The workmen rushed to the place where Prokhor fell, expecting to find him dead. But they found him

quite unharmed. This was the first of many miracles that occurred to him.

In 1769, at the age of ten, Prokhor became
seriously ill, and had to interrupt his education.
One night, as he lay in his bed, he saw the All-
Holy Theotokos in a vision. She spoke to him
and promised to make him well. Some days later,
he was carried by his mother to the miracle-working icon of the Theotokos of Kursk to venerate it.
Soon after this he recovered from his illness and
resumed his education. This miraculous cure was
the second miracle in the Saint's life, while the
vision of the Theotokos was first of a dozen visions
in which she appeared to him during his lifetime.

The miraculous cure marked the beginning of
a life of very ardent devotion to God and the
Church. Prokhor became an avid reader of the
Holy Scriptures and the lives of saints, and a frequent churchgoer.

When he was seventeen years old, Prokhor began to work as a partner at his brother's store in
Kursk. But he did not like this occupation. He
continued to attend church regularly, and to read
the Bible and the lives of saints, especially the
Desert Fathers.

As a result of reading these sacred texts, he began to aspire to become a monk. Accordingly, when he was eighteen, he set out to visit the Monastery of Pechersk, or the Monastery of the Caves, at Kiev. This monastery was founded in the 11th century by Antony Pechersky and his disciple Theodosius.[1] Here, he was advised by the Abbot to go to the Monastery of Sarov and stay there, for that place would help him attain salvation. The Sarov monastery was about 350 miles from Kursk.

In 1778, having obtained the consent of his mother, Prokhor left his native town and went to Sarov. He was received into the monastery by Abbot Pakhomius on November 20th, the eve of the Presentation of the Theotokos in the Temple. As a novice, he showed great fervor, humility, and obedience. He fulfilled the discipline of the monastery very diligently, participating regularly in the common worship, chanting, fasting, and performing conscientiously the various tasks that were assigned to him. In addition he read regularly the Holy Scriptures, the lives of saints, and the writings of the Eastern Fathers, such as the *Spiritual Homilies* of St. Macarios the Great, the *Hexae-meron* of St. Basil the Great, the *Ladder* of St.

John Climacos, and the *Discourses* of St. Isaac the
Syrian and St. Symeon the New Theologian. Further, he practiced mental prayer, or prayer of the
heart, particularly in the form known as the Jesus
Prayer: "Lord Jesus Christ, Son of God, have
mercy upon me, a sinner."

After two years of monastic life led with excessive austerities, his health was undermined: he
developed dropsy and had to be confined to bed.
In 1783, he became well following a vision of the
Theotokos, in which she appeared with the Apostles Peter and John, and laid her hand on him.
This was the second time the Virgin appeared
to him.

On August 13, 1786, after nearly seven years
as a novice, Prokhor was tonsured a monk by
Abbot Pakhomius, and was renamed Seraphim.

In October of the same year, at the age of twenty-
seven, he was ordained deacon. He served as a
deacon for seven years with extraordinary piety
and dedication, and was deemed worthy of supernatural visions. Thus, at times he saw angels taking part in the church services, and once he saw
Christ Himself.

At the age of thirty-four, St. Seraphim was ordained priest. He served in this capacity, too, with great fervor.

A year after his ordination to the priesthood, in 1794, following the death of Abbot Pakhomius, St. Seraphim asked the new Abbot, Father Isaac, for permission to withdraw to a hermitage. The hermit's way of life has traditionally been considered by the Orthodox as one making possible higher spiritual attainments, for those who are duly prepared, than life in a monastery. As we have noted, St. Seraphim practiced mental prayer from the time he was a novice; and he realized that he could practice it with greater success in the absolute solitude and quiet provided by a hermitage. Permission was granted, and on November 20, the anniversary of his arrival at the monastery, the holy Father withdrew to a hut in the woods, about three and a half miles from the monastery. The hut was on a hill, which he named Mount Athos, an indication of his very high opinion of the Holy Mountain of Athos. He dedicated his hut to the All-Holy Virgin, whose icon he placed inside it. In his biographies this icon is said to have been of the type called the "Virgin of Compassion" (*Umileniye*).[2]

Here he led a very austere mode of life. He
fasted to a far greater extent than is required by
the canons of the Church, prayed continuously,
read the Scriptures, especially the Gospels, and
the writings of the Fathers, and worked at his
vegetable garden as well as in the forest, where he
felled trees and chopped wood. He chanted various hymns as he worked, following in this the
counsel given by St. Basil, St. Theodore the Stu-
dite, and other great teachers of the monastic life.
On Saturdays, he would go to the monastery for
the evening services, and stay there for the Divine
Liturgy on Sunday morning, when he partook
of the Holy Eucharist.

In September of 1804, after nearly ten years as
a hermit, the Saint was badly beaten by three
brutal men who were in search of supposed hid-
den treasures in the region where he lived. Although very seriously injured, he succeeded in
dragging himself to the monastery. While in the
infirmary of the monastery, he saw the All-Holy
Virgin, accompanied by the Apostles Peter and
John. She told him that there was no need of doctors. This was his third vision of the Theotokos.
He thereupon entered a state of ineffable bliss
which continued for four hours. After this he
began to recover.

When he returned to his hermitage some months later, after he had become well enough, St. Seraphim found a new settler living not far from it: Hieromonk Nazarus (d. 1809). This monk had been one of the editors of the *Dobrotolubiye,* the Slavonic version of the famous *Philokalia,*[3] made by Paissy Velichkovsky (1722-1794) and published in 1793 at Petersburg. Having settled here, Nazarus practiced inner stillness—*hesychia,* as it is called in the *Philokalia*—and prayer of the heart. In all probability, St. Seraphim was already acquainted with this publication and began at this time to study it more assiduously, after listening to what Nazarus had told him about it. The influence of the *Dobrotolubiye* is manifest in his *Spiritual Counsels,* where he speaks of important practices that are taught in it, such as inner stillness, guarding of the heart, and mental prayer. It is also evident in his *Conversation* with his disciple Nicholas Motovilov, where the central theme is the purpose of human life. This is said to be—as is repeatedly stressed in the *Philokalia*—*theosis,* union with God, the fullest possible participation in Divine grace.

One would think that upon his return to his hermitage, after the brutal beating which he had

received, he would have eased somewhat his austere mode of life. But the exact opposite took
place. He began a three-year period of *standing.*
At night, he stood on a very large stone half way
between his cell and the monastery. He prayed
on this stone, either standing or kneeling. In day-
time, he continued this practice on a stone inside
his cell, from morning till nightfall. This kind of
discipline may have been undertaken as part of
his way of overcoming the assaults of demons.[4] In
the light of his teaching, it was also intended as an
aid to attaining positive higher states. Thus, at a
later time he remarked that "one must read the
New Testament and the Psalter standing, for this
helps one attain illumination of the rational fac-
ulty and heavenly transformation."[5]

In 1807, St. Seraphim began a period of *complete silence,* which he was to continue until 1820.
He spoke to no one and answered no questions.
He undertook this practice because he believed
it would lead to definitive victory over the devil,
complete inner peace, and many other gifts of the
Holy Spirit. That he believed that silence is conducive to these ends can be seen from what he says
in his *Spiritual Counsels.*

On May 8, 1810, the holy Father returned to

the Monastery of Sarov, in compliance with the request of the new Abbot, Niphont, who did not approve of his life as a hermit. The following day he shut himself up in the cell which he had occupied before. There he continued his practice of silence, and commenced the way of enclosure, of the "recluse." He permitted no one to enter his cell, except the nurse and the priest. The latter brought him Holy Communion every Sunday and on all feast days, after the Divine Liturgy. But he did not speak even to them. The confinement was not absolute, for, besides permitting entry to these two monks, at night he would go out of his cell and take a short walk around the main church of the monastery or towards the nearby cemetery. However, he never went out of his cell by day. He occupied himself with prayer and reading. At times he had visions of angels.

St. Seraphim's enclosure was relaxed somewhat in September, 1815. He opened his door and allowed monks to enter his cell. This form of confinement he practiced for a period of ten years.

On November 25, 1825, the All-Holy Virgin appeared to the Saint and gave him permission to end his confinement, break his silence, and devote

himself to his fellow men. Henceforth, he was to
serve as a healer, comforter, and Spiritual Guide,
Starets. The exercise of this vocation was not to be
continuous. He obtained permission from Abbot
Niphont to divide his time between the monastery
and a Near Hermitage, about two miles from the
monastery. A hut was built for him there, near a
spring with therapeutic water, where the Theotokos had once appeared to him. He now spent
Sundays and feast days at the monastery, and
Wednesdays and Fridays at the Near Hermitage,
devoting himself wholly to prayer.

During this period of *starchestvo,* as a Starets,
which was to continue until his repose, he performed many miracles of healing. The first such
miracle took place a little earlier, in 1823. It consisted in healing a young man named Michael
Manturov, who became one of his most dedicated
disciples. From 1825 on one cure followed another. The deaf gained their hearing, the blind
their sight, the paralyzed the ability to move; the
possessed found themselves free from demonic influence. The most famous healing of the Saint was
that of Nicholas Motovilov, another very dedicated
disciple, to whom the Starets gave the name *Friend
of God (Bogolyubye)*. Motovilov was suffering

from severe rheumatism that had paralyzed his legs. This miracle took place in 1831, two years before the repose of the Saint.

Besides persons who came to the Monastery of Sarov to be healed by St. Seraphim, there were great numbers of others who came to be comforted morally or materially, or to receive his counsel. Towards all—young and old, men and women—he showed profound compassion and Christian love, and offered them effective assistance.

Most important of all, he offered people spiritual guidance, instructing persons in the ways that lead to the acquisition of Divine grace, to union with God, to salvation. As a Spiritual Guide, a Starets, he sometimes heard confession. But this was not often; usually he sent people to the appointed confessors of the Monastery of Sarov, even though he had the gift of confession, for he could read the secret thoughts and deeds of people.

The first whom the Saint served as a Spiritual Guide were the women who lived in a religious community at Diveyevo, a small village seven miles from Sarov. He assumed an active role in the care of this community in 1823. The following year, heeding an order which he received from the

Theotokos, he formed in its proximity another religious community, consisting of nuns who supported themselves by working a mill that was built through his initiative. He directed this community too. St. Seraphim served also as Spiritual Guide of countless other persons who came to him. The best known of these were the laymen Manturov and Motovilov who, as we have already noted, had been healed by him. The spiritual teaching which he gave to Motovilov has been preserved in *A Conversation with Saint Seraphim* which Motovilov wrote and which was published posthumously.

During the last period of his life, two new remarkable things about him were noticed: his face was sometimes seen lit by a dazzling supernatural light, and on several occasions he was seen levitating—standing or walking above the ground. Thus, Ivan Meliukov, whose sister Mary belonged to the religious community at Diveyevo, once saw his face "lit by so dazzling a light that he could not look at him without shielding his eyes."[6] Among others who are said to have seen him in this state of illumination were the nun Matrona and Nicholas Motovilov. Matrona is reported to have said that once, as she looked at the holy Starets, she "was dazzled by the sight of his face, which seemed full of light and like an angel's."[7] In the already mentioned *Conversation,* Motovilov has given the most detailed account that we have of the appearance of the Starets in this state of grace.

With regard to *levitation,* we read in the lives of St. Seraphim that he was once seen by some nuns of Diveyevo walking about in a meadow a yard above the ground. We also read that on another occasion, while the Saint was in his cell at the monastery praying for a sick man who lay on a bed inside the cell, the man saw him standing in mid-air. The Starets told those who happened to see him in this state not to tell anyone about it as long as he lived.[8]

On March 24, 1831, St. Seraphim had his twelfth and last vision of the Theotokos. While in his cell, he saw the All-Holy Virgin escorted by two angels, the Apostles Peter and John, and twelve virgin martyrs. The vision lasted about four hours. At the end she said to the Starets: "Soon, my dear one, you shall be with us." He took this statement to mean that his death would take place in the near future, and began making preparations for his departure from this life, even giving directions about his burial.

His repose occurred in the morning of January 2nd, 1833, as he was praying in his cell. It brought great sorrow to all who knew him. Persons came from all quarters to pay their last respects to him. His body was exposed in the main church of the monastery for a whole week in a coffin which he himself had made.

Seraphim's reputation among the common people as well as among intellectuals and official persons, including the imperial family, grew in the period that followed his repose. Among intellectuals who are known to have been influenced by him was the philosopher Ivan Kireyevsky (1806-1856). It was through his wife Natalia, who had been a spiritual daughter of the Starets, that Kireyevsky returned to Orthodoxy.

Along with the spreading of St. Seraphim's reputation, there was an increasing number of reports of miracles performed by him. A commission which had been appointed by the Holy Synod of the Church of Russia reported in 1892 that it had found about 100 miracles, most of them miraculous cures, attributed to the Starets.

Official recognition of Seraphim as a Saint came from the Church of Russia on July 19, 1903, on the anniversary of his birth, seventy years after his death. Since then his memory is celebrated by the Russian Orthodox and by other Orthodox Christians on January 2, the day of his repose, and on July 19, with special services in which many uplifting hymns are chanted in his honor, such as the following kontakion:

"Having left the beauty of the world and what is corrupt therein, O Saint, thou didst settle in Sarov Monastery. And having lived there an angelic life, thou wast for many the way unto salvation. Wherefore, Christ hath glorified thee, O Father Seraphim, and hath enriched thee with the gift of healing and miracles. Therefore we cry to thee: Rejoice, O Seraphim, our righteous Father."

II

Admiration for St. Seraphim has steadily grown since the time when he was officially recognized as a Saint. Simultaneously with this phenomenon there have arisen some misunderstandings about his place in the Orthodox tradition of spirituality. Thus, one writer tells us that he sees in St. Seraphim "one of those Adepts who stand outside tradition, orthodoxy, dogma, and history."[10] An-

other writer observes that St. Seraphim "was the
forerunner of the new form of spirituality which
should succeed merely ascetical monasticism;"
that he was "the white, spirit-bearing flame of
mystical prayer . . . , which should succeed the
black night of austerity."[11] And another author
says that the Saint's "intimacy with the Mother
of God which is discernible throughout his life . . .
is a singular example of both predilection on
Mary's part and of veneration on his;"[12] and that
"when he forsook the extreme form of hermit life
and returned to the world he may be said to have
passed beyond institutional monasticism. . . ."[13]

Such statements are unwarranted. When carefully related to the long Orthodox tradition of
monasticism, the facts about St. Seraphim show
him to have been an authentic follower of it, one
who never abandoned this tradition, and always
stood within the borders of Orthodoxy in general.

It was noted earlier that St. Seraphim had a
very high opinion of Mount Athos—that great
Orthodox community of monasteries, sketes and
hermitages which has a history of over a thousand
years—as is shown by the fact that he named the
hill on which his Distant Hermitage was located

Mount Athos. Having been an avid reader of lives of saints, he undoubtedly knew that two of the most remarkable Russian saints, Antony Pechersky (d. 1073) and Nilus Sorsky (*c.* 1433-1508), owed an enormous debt to the Holy Mountain of Athos. St. Antony received at Athos the Great and Angelic Habit, and dwelt there for many years. Later he returned to Russia and founded the first great Russian monastery, the Pecherskaya Lavra or Monastery of the Caves, which St. Seraphim visited before he went to Sarov.[14] St. Nilus spent several years at Athos, and upon returning to his native land made it his special mission in life to teach the spiritual ideas and practices of Athonite monasticism, such as guarding of the mind, spiritual combat, meditation, concentration, and mental prayer—a form of prayer which St. Seraphim practiced from the time he was a novice to the end of his life. Nilus also introduced into Russia the sketic form of monastic life which he had observed on Mount Athos—a form half way between life in a monastery and the life of the solitary hermit.[15] Fedotov remarks that "Seraphim seems like a contemporary and the closest spiritual relation of Nilus Sorsky."[16] This kinship was not a matter of chance, but a result of knowledge of the life and teaching of St. Nilus on the part of

St. Seraphim. The holy Father was also aware of the debt another important Russian monastic leader, his older contemporary Paissy Velichkovsky, owed to Athos. Paissy dwelt there for seventeen years. Afterward he settled in Moldavia (part of present day Rumania), and with his disciples effected a spiritual revival there and in Russia. One of Paissy's collaborators, Nazarus, as we have already noted, settled in 1804 near St. Seraphim's hermitage; and at that time, if not earlier, the Saint must have learned a great deal about Paissy, his activities, monastic ideals and practices.

In the "Fragments from the Life of Saint Seraphim," contained in Fedotov's *A Treasury of Russian Spirituality*, there is a passage which appears to contradict the thesis that St. Seraphim had very high esteem for Athonite monasticism. We read: "Many came to Father Seraphim to ask his blessing and his approval for their intention of retiring to Mount Athos for the salvation of their soul. But the Starets refused to grant his blessing to any one of them, saying that things were very difficult and unutterably dull there. In his opinion it was most convenient to seek salvation in Orthodox Russia."[17] It must be observed that this statement was made by St. Seraphim during his period as a Starets, which was between 1825 and 1833. At that time things were indeed very difficult and dull on Athos, because following the outbreak of the Greek War of Independence on March 25, 1821, the Holy Mountain was occupied by 3,000 Turkish soldiers, who stayed there until 1829. Their presence resulted in the departure of 5,000 of the 6,000 monks, and the imposition upon the remaining monks of the heavy burden of feeding and paying this occupation army. It took many years for life there to return to normal.

Such practices as fasting, vigils, standing during church services and during private prayer, and silence, which are among the features that characterize Athonite monasticism and Orthodox monasticism in general, are conspicuous in the life of St. Seraphim from the time he was a novice at the Monastery of Sarov to the time of his repose. If these and other similar practices of Orthodox monasticism constitute "the black night of austerity," it was a "night" from which the Saint never emerged or suggested that monasticism should emerge from, in order to cultivate "the new form of spirituality." It should be added that the characterization "black night" is most inappropriate for a tradition of monasticism whose fruits have been the attainment of Divine light, spiritual health, joy, love and peace.

Certain experiences of St. Seraphim, as well as certain of his practices, either have been viewed, or will be viewed, by some as unique or as foreign to Orthodox monasticism and Orthodoxy in general. This must be attributed to insufficient acquaintance with traditional Orthodox spirituality.

The Saint's intimacy with the Theotokos has been noted in this Introductory. One writer, as we saw, calls it "singular." But other examples of such intimacy may be found in the lives of Orthodox saints. Thus, in the life of St. Athanasios the Athonite (10th century), founder of the first monastery on Athos, that of Lavra, we read that "he had great reverence for the Ever-Virgin and most glorious Theotokos, and was deemed worthy of seeing her often, even with his physical eyes, as he saw her also with his spiritual eyes."[18] In the life of another holy monk of Athos, the great cantor, hymnographer and music theorist John Koukouzelis (12th century), we read this: "Once, on the Saturday of the Akathistos Hymn, after he had chanted carefully the Idiomela and the Canon of the Theotokos as he was accustomed to do, he went into a momentary trance while he stood in his stall. Then there appeared the Lady Theotokos and she said to him: 'Rejoice, John, my child; chant to me and I shall not abandon you.' Having said this, she gave him a gold coin. When he awoke, he found, miraculously, the coin in his right hand. Filled with infinite joy, he thanked the Mother of God. This coin they placed in the church, and it performed great wonders. From that time St. John was never absent from the right choir, but chanted eagerly and glorified the Lord tirelessly. From his great efforts and long standing his legs rotted and emitted fetid matter; but the Virgin healed him, as she had healed John Damascene. She appeared to him and said: 'You shall be from now on healthy;' and immediately he was completely healed. Wherefore he thanked the Mother of God and remained free of sickness until the end of his life.''[19] Another example of a remarkable relation with the Theotokos is found in the life of St. Maximos Kafsokalyvitis, who, like Athanasios and John Koukouzelis, led a life of spiritual endeavor on Mount Athos. In his life that appears in the *New Eklogion* of Nicodemos the Hagiorite, the following incidents are related. "Once, on the Sunday of the Holy Fathers, which comes after the divine Ascension, the Theotokos appeared to him, bearing in her arms the Lord,

and said to him: 'Follow me, most faithful Maximos, and climb up Athos, in order to receive the
grace of the Holy Spirit, as you desire.' Having
seen this vision a second and a third time, he left
the Monastery of Great Lavra, and after seven
days, on Saturday of Pentecost, he reached the
top of the Mountain. The divine Maximos remained there for three days and three nights,
praying unceasingly to God and to the Theotokos, employing mental prayer. . . . Having
prayed thus, there appeared to him the Theotokos in great glory, as a queen, surrounded by
many angels, again holding in her arms her Son,
the Creator of the whole universe. Convinced
from that overwhelming Divine light which shone
and illuminated everything in that region, and assured that it was not a demonic delusion but a
divine vision and a true manifestation of the
Theotokos, he glorified her with inexpressible
joy, saying: 'Hail, thou who art full of grace, the
Lord is with thee;' and the like. Then he pro-
strated himself and venerated the Lord and the
Theotokos, received the blessing of the Lord, and
heard the All-Holy Virgin saying: 'Receive the gift
against demons, thou venerable prize-bearer, and
settle at the foot of the peak of Athos; for this is
the will of my Son, in order that you may ascend

to the heights of virtue, and become the teacher and guide of many and save them.' After this there was given to him heavenly bread as food and refreshment of his nature, as he had been without food for so many days. As soon as he took the bread and put it in his mouth, he was surrounded by Divine light from above, and he heard an Angelic hymn, and thus the Theotokos rose to the heavenly realm."[20] In the same life we are told that from the time of his youth Maximos Kafsokalyvitis had great faith in the All-Holy Virgin, and prayed fervently to her to give him the gift of mental prayer, and how his persistent supplication found response. Maximos is quoted as having said: "One day, as I kissed with love her holy icon, I at once felt in my breast and in my heart a warmth and flame that came from the holy icon. It did not burn me, but refreshed and sweetened me, and brought to my heart great contrition. From that time on, my heart began to say within it the prayer, and my intellect to be sweetened by the remembrance of Jesus and the Theotokos, and to maintain always remembrance of them."[21]

Levitation is another phenomenon in the life of St. Seraphim that some will consider unique in Orthodoxy. But here again one will find other in-

stances in the lives of the saints. In the life of
Hosios Lukas (*ca.* 896-946/953)—the Saint to
whom there was dedicated the magnificent 11th
century Byzantine church at Steiri in Boeotia—
we read that his mother saw him on three different
occasions standing at prayer elevated more than
two feet above the ground. It is added that other
persons, too, had seen Hosios Lukas praying in
this manner.[22] Niketas Stethatos (11th century)
cites two instances when St. Symeon the New
Theologian (949-1022), the greatest of Byzantine
mystics, was seen at prayer about eight feet above
the floor of his cell. A disciple of Symeon, named
Nikephoros, related the following instance, according to Stethatos: "Near the ceiling of the cell
[of St. Symeon] there hung an icon of the Theotokos called *Deesis,* in front of which there burned
a holy lamp. One night, I saw the Saint directly
opposite this icon, about eight feet (four *pecheis*)
above the ground. He stood in the air, with his
hands lifted and praying, all brilliant, like light.
. . . At dawn, I narrated the incident to the Saint
when no one else was present. The Saint sighed
and ordered me not to tell about it to anyone."[23]
The other occasion cited by Stethatos was again
witnessed by Nikephoros. It took place during the
time when Symeon was near the point of death

and lay in bed, incapable of getting up or turning around.[24] Among other Orthodox saints who have been observed in a state of levitation is the already mentioned Hagiorite monk Maximos Kafsokalyvitis.[25]

The external, objective, side of illumination is another manifestation of St. Seraphim that needs to be seen in historical perspective. Those not familiar with the long tradition of Orthodox spirituality perhaps will think that it is something unique. In the *Conversation* which he had with the Saint, Motovilov says that as he was talking with Seraphim about the acquisition of the grace of the Holy Spirit, the Saint's face suddenly became bright as the sun. This phenomenon has been observed in many other Orthodox saints. In his *Leimon,* "Meadow," the monk John Moschos (7th century) says that the recluse Hosios David of Thessaloniki emitted light while inside his hut. Those who happened to be in the environs of the hut saw the light at night in the form of flames coming out of all the windows. The flames were seen again and again by many persons, including the soldiers who were guarding the city walls. At first it was thought that the hut had been set afire by the barbarians.[26] In *Evergetinos,*[27] there is

this story about the Desert Father Abba Sisoes:
When he was about to die, the monks who
sat about him noticed that his face shone very
brightly, and this brightness went on increasing
until suddenly his face became like the sun.[28] Symeon the New Theologian, as we have already
noted, was seen by one of his disciples all bright
as he prayed above the ground. In his life by Stethatos it is said also that often, as St. Symeon offi-
ciated at the Divine Liturgy, his face was seen
bright and angelic, so much so that one could
hardly look at it owing to its brightness.[29]

With regard to St. Seraphim's practices of standing, silence, and confinement, it should be remarked that these are parts of the traditional way
of the *hesychast,* the Orthodox mystic, except that
for a period of time the holy Father practiced
them in an extreme form. In his practice of standing on a rock over a period of three years, he was
inspired by the example of the stylites of old, as
well as by that of some of the Desert Fathers and
by the writings of the Byzantine hesychasts. His
choice of a three-year period may have been inspired by one of the early Egyptian hermits named
John, who at the beginning of his life in the desert
spent "three years below a rock always praying,

without sitting at all, and without sleeping, except for the little sleep which he could snatch as he stood."[30] St. Seraphim's three-year period was not so severe as that of John, for the Russian hermit spent it alternately standing and kneeling. The value of standing—although not in such an extreme form—is stressed by great ascetic-mystical Fathers such as Hesychios of Jerusalem (5th century), John Climacos (7th century), Theodore of Edessa (7th century), Symeon the New Theologian (11th century), Gregory the Sinaite (14th century), and many others. They include it among the physical practices, and hold that it assists in withering the bodily passions and preventing overt sinning. St. Gregory the Sinaite teaches that to spend all the night in vigil and standing (*stasis*) is part of the way of the perfect.[31]

Much is to be found in the works of the Fathers just mentioned about the value of silence for the hesychast. In Climacos' *Ladder of Divine Ascent* silence (*siope*) is the eleventh of thirty steps of ascent to spiritual perfection. He calls silence "the mother of prayer, . . . a companion of quiet, a creator of contemplation, unseen progress, secret ascent."[32] Again, he says: "The friend of silence draws near to God, and by secretly conversing with Him, is enlightened by God."[33] By silence, St. John and the other Fathers do not mean the complete avoidance of talking which was practiced by St. Seraphim over a period of thirteen years—although they do not proscribe it, for many saintly hermits lived for years without seeing anyone and hence without talking at all for years. They mean rather the avoidance of unnecessary talking. This form of silence Seraphim always observed. Commending such silence, Diadochos of Photike (mid-fifth century) says: "Goodness always flees from talkativeness, being alien to all agitation and phantasy. Seasonable silence is, then, beautiful, being nothing other than the mother of very wise thoughts."[34] And Gregory the Sinaite, stressing its great value for inner stillness, remarks: "He who practices stillness (*hesychia*) must have first of all, as a foundation, these virtues: silence, self-restraint, vigils, humility, and patience."[35]

Also, the life of confinement which St. Seraphim led at the monastery for fifteen years is not something new in Orthodox monasticism. In Greek ascetic and hagiographical literature it is called the life of the *enkleistos,* and the cell, hut, or cave where one leads this life is called an *enkleisterion* or *enkleistria.* In English language writings it is called the life of a "recluse" or the life of "enclosure." In adopting this practice, like that of the "stylite," the Saint apparently was inspired by accounts contained in the writings about the Desert Fathers of Egypt and elsewhere. St. John of Lykos, one of the Egyptian hermits, is said to have lived in a cave for forty years without ever having gone out of it, or anyone having entered it. He received through a small window a little food that others brought to him.[36] Another Egyptian hermit, Abba Theon, is said to have lived as a recluse in a hut for thirty years.[37] St. Barsanouphios, one of the great masters of the spiritual life, is said to have lived shut up in a very small cell in Gaza for fifty years without having been seen by anyone, except once.[38] Among recluses of a later date is Neophytos the Recluse, of Cyprus. Born in 1134, he became one of the great ascetics of Cyprus. He built his *enkleistria* and spent his whole life inside it in prayer and study.[39] The practice of confinement is intended to reduce distractions and agitation to a minimum, making it easy to practice pure mental prayer.

One more practice of the Saint about which something should be said is that of frequent Holy

Communion. He always stressed the importance of this practice to the people who came to him, and he urged priests to facilitate it. He said: "So great is the grace received through the Holy Mysteria, that it has the power to purify and regenerate every man, no matter how great a sinner he may be."[40] In practicing and urging frequent Holy Communion, the Starets again stood firmly in the Orthodox Tradition. This can be verified if one reads the book *Concerning Continual Communion,* which was written by St. Macarios of Corinth and was expanded and translated into simple phraseology by St. Nicodemos the Hagiorite.[41] Making use of passages from the New Testament, the writings of the Eastern Fathers, and the Canons of the Apostles and of the Ecumenical Synods, the book shows: (a) that it is necessary for the Orthodox to partake often of the Body and Blood of our Lord; (b) that continual Communion is beneficial and conducive to salvation; and (c) that delay in receiving Communion causes one great harm.

In his emphasis on, and practice of, frequent Communion and mental prayer, as well as in his predilection for the writings of the ascetic-mystical Fathers, such as Saints Macarios the Great,

Isaac the Syrian, John Climacos, Maximos the Confessor, and Symeon the New Theologian, St. Seraphim is akin to his Greek contemporaries known as *Kollyvades*.[42] Prominent among the latter were Macarios of Corinth and Nicodemos the Hagiorite. They were very influential not only through the just mentioned book *Concerning Continual Communion,* but also through the *Philokalia,* which was compiled by Macarios and edited by Nicodemos.

The holy Father resembles also in several respects another of his older Greek contemporaries, St. Cosmas Aitolos. Both had the gift of miracles. Both had the gift of foretelling the future. Both stressed the importance of Baptism. Cosmas asserted in his sermons that it is impossible for an unbaptized man to be saved; and added that to be properly baptized one had to be fully immersed, and this called for large baptismal basins. To this end he urged his listeners to buy such basins and donate them to churches which did not possess them. In his *Conversation* with his disciple Motovilov, Seraphim similarly dwells on the importance of Baptism, asserting that the grace of the Holy Spirit is given in this Sacrament, and that this grace is very great and indispensible for

man. Again, neither saint wrote anything for publication. The publications which convey their oral
teachings were written by their disciples and appeared posthumously. Finally, both lived for
many years far from people of the "world," but
later came in close touch with great multitudes.
St. Cosmas dwelt at the Monastery of Philotheou
on Mount Athos for seventeen years, and then,
having obtained the consent and blessing of his
elders at the monastery, went into the world and
served for nineteen years as an itinerant spiritual
awakener and teacher of the true faith. Preaching
in Constantinople, in many parts of Greece and
in Albania, he brought about a profound inner
transformation in countless souls. St. Seraphim,
after living for many years as a hermit and then
in self-imposed confinement at the Monastery of
Sarov, made himself available to multitudes of pilgrims who came to the monastery to be healed by
him, to be comforted, or to receive spiritual counsel. He served in this capacity effectively during
the last eight years of his life. Both succeeded in
effecting the inner transformation of large multitudes: Father Cosmas by returning to the world,
without ever becoming of it, and Father Seraphim
by remaining at the monastery but letting the
world come to him.

III

The teaching of St. Seraphim, as it is conveyed in his *Conversation* with Motovilov and in his *Spiritual Counsels*, is traditional Orthodox teaching, free of heterodox elements.

The central idea in the *Conversation* is that the supreme aim of man should be the acquisition of the grace of the Holy Spirit. This is the traditional Orthodox view that the goal of man should be *theosis*, "deification" or "divinization," that is, union with God through grace, participation in His perfection and blessedness. It is presented by St. Seraphim with the same emphasis that we find in the *Spiritual Homilies* of Macarios the Great, the *Discourses* of Symeon the New Theologian, and the writings of other great Eastern Fathers. The interpretation of the parable of the five wise and the five foolish virgins that is used to illustrate his teaching on the acquisition of Divine grace is taken from Macarios' fourth homily. His discussion of the point that at the descent of the Holy Spirit in the soul one should be completely still even to prayer is reminiscent of what St. Maximos Kafsokalyvitis says on this subject in a text contained in the *Philokalia*.[43]

In the *Conversation,* the Saint also speaks of the

various means whereby grace is acquired: the Mysteria ("Sacraments") of Holy Baptism, Chrismation and Communion, prayer, vigils, fasting, alms-
giving and the other virtues. The *Conversation*
contains in addition a description of the external
manifestations of the acquisition of grace and the
inner experiences of him who acquires it.

Furthermore, the *Conversation* contains references to the Holy Trinity, to God as creator, almighty, ruler of all and providence; to the enemy
of mankind, the devil; to the nature of man, as
constituted of soul and body; and to other important topics.

In the *Spiritual Counsels,* the chief subjects discussed are God; the virtues of hope, love, patience,
humility; care of the soul; the practices of fasting,
silence, guarding of the heart, and prayer. Everything said here can be found in the *Philokalia* and
other works containing the teaching of great
ascetic-mystical Fathers of the Orthodox Church.

The topic of the afterlife, which is central in
Orthodoxy, is not discussed, either in the *Conversation* or in the *Spiritual Counsels.* Firm belief in
it, however, is conveyed by St. Seraphim's whole
orientation in life, which was otherworldly, and

by certain remarks contained in accounts of his life. Thus, some days before his death, he said: "In body, I already feel dead to all, but in spirit I feel as strong as if I were newly born." Again, he observed: "What joy, what delights await the soul when the angels of God come to fetch it!"[44]

THE LIFE OF ST. SERAPHIM

By Mary-Barbara Zeldin

Of all Russian saints, Seraphim of Sarov is particularly dear to every Russian Orthodox today. There are several reasons for this. One is that his teaching spread to all parts of Russia, marking the beginning of a new religious consciousness in an age of growing materialism. Another is that he appears as an embodiment of all that is meant by Russian spirituality. And a third is that his life seems to synthesize all the ways by which a soul can rise to God.[1] That Orthodox Christianity has survived in Russia in this century amid the persecutions it has endured, and the suffering of the faithful, is explicable in good part by the fact that Russia is a country which could produce such a Saint, and by the inspiration and example of persons like him.

St. Seraphim was born in Kursk, a provincial town in Great Russia near the Ukrainian border, some 300 miles south of Moscow, on July 19, 1759,[2] the son of Isidore and Agatha Moshnin. At Holy Baptism he was given the name of Prokhor.[3] His family lived in comfortable circumstances, for his father owned a brick factory and was also a building contractor.

When Prokhor was only three years old, his father died, while in charge of the construction of a church for Kursk. Prokhor's mother, a capable and determined woman, took over his work. She supervised the construction during the twelve year period that was needed for the completion of the edifice.[4] She also took charge of the factory until Prokhor's elder brother, Alexei, was old enough to take over its management. In addition, she not only did everything possible to bring up her children in a truly Christian manner, but also took into her home orphan girls of the town and even provided doweries and found suitable husbands for them.

The devout mother was soon to receive indications of Prokhor's destined vocation. The first came when the boy was seven years old. During a routine visit with his mother to the church that was under construction, the boy climbed and slipped from the top of the scaffolding that surrounded the seven-storey bell-tower. From such a height he would normally have been critically injured or even killed. Prokhor got up unharmed. Three years later, he fell very seriously ill. One day during his illness, he told his mother of a dream he had just experienced: the All-Holy Virgin had appeared to him and told him that she would personally come to cure him. A few days later, on the occasion of a religious festival, the miracle-working icon of Our Lady of Kursk was being carried through the town in procession when, as the procession passed the Moshnin house, a sudden cloudburst drove the people to seek shelter for the icon within the house yard. Prokhor's mother, Agatha, brought the child to the icon to venerate it. He was cured the same day. It is said that at another time, a "fool for Christ"[5] — as certain holy men are known among the Orthodox — stopped Agatha and Prokhor on the street and said, prophetically, to the young widow: "You are fortunate, for you have a son who will become a mighty intercessor before the Holy Spirit, a man of prayer for the entire world."

The boy was "in this world, but never of it."[6] He showed himself assiduous and gifted in all his studies, but his favorite reading material was religious: the Lives of Saints, the *Psalter*, the *Horologion*, the Gospels, and other religious writings. He became friends with the "fool for Christ" whom he had met as a small child on the street. And, partly at this man's suggestion, he went on a pilgrimage to Kiev when he was eighteen, accompanied by five other youths, to pray at the graves of the Pechersky saints Anthony and Fyodor for guidance as to his future life. He received his answer through the aged Starets[7] or Spiritual Father Dosithei, who approved the youth's desire for a religious life, and directed him to the Monastery of Sarov. "Go, child of God," Father Dosithei said, "and remain there. This place will ensure your salvation . . . . Seek only to achieve the constant consciousness of God by continual appeal to His name, and the Holy Spirit will be implanted in you and will direct your life to what is blessed."[8]

Prokhor was overjoyed. Several of his fellow townsmen had already gone to Sarov and it was there that he, too, was longing to go.

The separation from his mother, to whom he was devoted, was painful for him, as it was for her. But it had long been evident to her that her

younger son took no interest in commercial life
and the business which his brother was now run-
ning, and that he was destined for one of quite
another sort.[9] Prokhor left Kursk wearing the octa-
gonal copper cross which his mother gave him
as a parting gift, and which he was to wear constantly for the remainder of his life. With two of
the companions of his pilgrimage to Kiev, he
travelled the 350 or so miles that separated Kursk
from Sarov.

The Monastery of Sarov was located some eighty
miles south of the city of Nizhnyi-Novgorod (now
Gorky) in northern Tambov province, on the
border of the province of Nizhnyi-Novgorod. It
was built in a clearing in a dense forest at the
confluence of the Satis and Sarovka rivers, near
the remains of a Tatar fortress that had been
abandoned in the late 15th century. The site was
not hospitable: the forest was populated with
numerous wild animals — foxes, moose, otter,
deer, and bears — and served as a refuge for brigands and outlaws. Nearby villagers penetrated
it only to collect firewood and honey from the
hives of the many bees that throve in it. Nevertheless, they were jealous of their right to the
forest, and they viewed the first outsider to settle
there — a monk named Theodosius, who came in

search of solitude in 1654[10] — with considerable suspicion. His arrival marks the origin of the monastery. Theodosius was succeeded by Guerassim, and in 1670 Guerassim was followed by the monk Ioann.[11] It was Ioann who actually founded the monastery. He gathered a small number of followers and set up a community with a simple and strict rule of poverty and manual labor for self-support. After receiving permission from the Russian Patriarch — the last one before the reinstitution of the Patriarchate in the present century[12] — with the aid of his followers he built a church. Such was the community's enthusiasm, that the simple wooden structure was completed within fifty days of receipt of the permission. It is said that a joyous pealing of bells was heard in the forest at its consecration, although no bells existed in the monastery or even in its vicinity.

The monastery survived and even prospered. This is perhaps as miraculous as the sound of the bells, for it was founded just as Peter the Great was about to bear down drastically on all forms of Russian religious life in favor of Western ways. The monastery even survived, under Father Ephraim, who succeeded Father Ioann (d. 1747), not only the attacks of brigands and the fires that usually plagued monasteries, but also the harsh

persecution of monasteries during the reign of
Catherine II.[13] Once again fortunate in its tim-
ing, in 1764 the coenobitic community requested
and received permission to become eremitic as
well.[14]

When Prokhor came to it, some seventy years
after its official founding, the Monastery of Sarov
was a well-established settlement. The wooden
church had been replaced by a stone one with
gilded cupolas, and the local peasants now looked
upon it with respect and gratitude for both its
spiritual and its material assistance. The simple,
hard-working life led by the monks, their religious
concern, and their charitable work — especially
during the famine of 1774-1775, when the peasants were reduced to eating the bark of trees
and the monastery had managed to feed several
hundred daily — had not only changed the attitude of the nearby villagers, but also spread
the fame of the monastery to distant provinces
and made it a place of pilgrimage.

It was in the jurisdiction of this monastery
that Prokhor was to pass the remainder of his
earthly existence. He arrived on November 20,
1778, the eve of the Feast of the Presentation of
the Theotokos in the Temple. The Abbot, Father

Pakhomius, who had succeeded Father Ephraim, was also a native of Kursk. He was at once impressed by the tall, broad-shouldered, blond young man with the amazing blue eyes and candid expression, and received him with kindness and affection.

Prokhor served his novitiate under the supervision of the monastery bursar, Father Joseph, and followed strictly the rule prescribed in the 4th century by St. Pachomios.[15]

Because of his strong build and great physical endurance, he was asked to work at some of the more physically demanding aspects of the monastery's life. He perfomed with enthusiasm whatever tasks were entrusted to him. But he excelled in carpentry, to such an extent, that he came to be known as "Prokhor the Carpenter." He was especially zealous in prayer, however, both common and private.

This devotion by no means precluded youthful cheerfulness, which made him popular with his fellow novices. Prokhor's life was full of joy, and he tried to impart it to his associates, cheering them by his very presence and occasional pleasantries, both in their work and especially in the evenings, when, tired after a long day of activity, they chanted in the choir. "Joy is not a sin," he told a sister of the Convent of Diveyevo in later years. "It drives away despondency (*uniniye*), the worst of all things, for that brings everything else along with it. When I was a novice and chanted in the choir, I was always joyous. And every time I came and saw how my colleagues were weary and sad, I would begin to cheer them. Then they no longer felt weary. To say something evil (*durnoye*) is wrong and should not be done, especially in the house of God, but to speak a friendly word, even a word which brings cheerfulness, so that everyone may always have a joyous spirit and not be dejected before the face of God, that is not a sin. . . . We have no reason to be sad, for Christ has conquered all. He has bestowed life upon Adam, freed Eve, and killed death."

This cheerfulness, characteristic of the years of his novitiate, was to develop into a permanent attitude of simple love, fellowship, and joy toward all God's creatures. In later years he would greet those who came to him by bowing low before them and referring to Orthodoxy's most joyous day, Easter, saying: "Christ, my joy, is risen." He would continue to address his visitors as "my joy." And he always spoke of the Theotokos as "the Joy of all joys." In thus greeting and addressing visitors, Prokhor was expressing what he saw and felt. He saw the image of God in every man, and the sight filled him with joy.

The novitiate, however, is not easy. Although Prokhor obviously enjoyed his companions and was popular among them, the joy was probably in part due to the very fact that he was successfully encountering the first trials of the life he had chosen for himself. He was a brother to his brothers, and he performed the tasks imposed upon him with enthusiasm. But his solitary devotions and reading had to continue far into the night to make up for the time he had thus expended. He not only read, as expected, the Holy Scriptures, standing before the icons, but he tried wholly to assimilate their meaning and to practice what they teach. In addition, he read widely of the Holy Fathers — St. Basil the Great, St. Macarios the Great, St. John Climacos, and other ascetic-mystical Fathers[16]—and the *Menaion* of St. Dmitri of Rostov.[17] He led a life of great austerity, sleeping only four hours a night and eating but once a day, and then sparingly. On Wednesdays and Fridays, with the permission of the Abbot, he abstained from all food and spent the day in meditation and prayer in the forest.

Of this period of monastic training he said later: "Until the age of thirty-five,[18] that is, for the first half of our earthly existence, great is the effort required to avoid evil and many are those who cannot manage to do so." In the following counsel to novices he gives us an insight into the difficulties of this early period:

"Whatever the way by which you came into this monastery, do not be discouraged: God is here. Monastic life is not easy. Do not consider giving up one monastery for another at your first disappointment. A novice must will to persevere. From the hour he enters the monastery to the day of his death the life of a monk is but a terrible struggle against the world, the flesh, and the devil."[19]

The overstrenuous life of spiritual endeavor of Prokhor — his extreme forms of fasting and insufficient rest — undermined his health. In 1780, at the age of twenty-one, he fell ill from a type of dropsy which grew steadily worse. He became weaker and weaker, until, after three years, he could no longer leave his bed. As his state became desperate, Abbot Pakhomius wished to call for medical help, even though this was frowned upon by monastic custom. Prokhor, however, requested instead a service of prayer for his return to health. When the service he had asked for was over, the monks came back to his cell to find him cured. Much later, he explained that while the monks were at prayer, the All-Holy Virgin had come to him accompanied by the Apostles Peter and John. Speaking to them, she remarked: "He is of our family." She then put her hand on his forehead, and with her sceptre she touched his side. Water flowed from the incision so created, and he was cured. Only a deep scar remained as evidence of the miraculous intervention.

As soon as he had fully recoverd his strength, Prokhor sought and received permission from the Abbot to leave the monastery in search of contributions to build an infirmary and chapel in thanksgiving for the restoration of his health. He traveled long distances to solicit the necessary funds. Some say that he went even as far as Kursk, where he received a large contribution from his family. In 1784, the foundations of the Church of Sts. Zosima and Savvas were laid. Prokhor himself made the cypress-wood altar, and from the time it was ready he worshipped there whenever possible. It was from there that seventy years after his death his relics were carried with

great ceremony to a tomb in the Church of the
Dormition of the Theotokos, the main church
of the monastery, on the occasion of the official
recognition of him as a Saint.

Eight years after his arrival at the monastery,
on August 13, 1786, at the age of twenty-seven,
Prokhor received the tonsure from Fathers Joseph
and Isaiah. Abbot Pakhomius, who had been
deeply impressed by the young man's ardent,
"seraphic" faith, gave him the name of Seraphim.[20]
A short time later, Seraphim was ordained deacon
by Bishop Victor of Vladimir.

St. Seraphim's real trials now began. His zeal
aroused the resentment of his fellow monks, and
his open accounts of his mystical experiences
were a source of irritation.[21] Before his ordination
to the diaconate, he was given the work of sex-
ton. At that time he hardly left the church
except for a few hours' rest. While a deacon, he
would prepare for the Sunday service by spend-
ing the previous night praying, motionless, in the
church. At times, when the choir chanted, he
saw angels taking part in the service. Clothed
in white, brilliant, they would traverse the church
chanting heavenly music. To this music, he said,
nothing could be compared, and it so transported

him that time was nothing to him, and the whole service fused into a vision of light and glory. Finally, one Holy Thursday, during its long and very solemn Liturgy of St. Basil, at the time of the Entrance with the Gospel, Seraphim suddenly stopped, motionless, and had to be supported back behind the iconostasis. There he remained silent and immobile for several hours. Afterward, he explained to his superiors what had happened. He said that he had suddenly seen our Lord Himself in His glory, attended by the heavenly hosts, entering the church by the western door and stopping before the iconostasis, where he was standing. Christ blessed the celebrants, bestowing a special blessing on him. Then He left by entering into His icon on the iconostasis.

The older monks listened attentively to St. Seraphim. But, more experienced than he, they cautioned him against visions in general and against pride in particular. Such caution was indeed wise with regard to St. Seraphim's fellow monks, who had not yet achieved the humility of the elders, but it was not needed for Seraphim himself. For he took his visions not as rewards for past efforts on his part, but as divine means to stimulate him to further, greater efforts; and even at this young age humility was one of his

outstanding characteristics. It was in good part
this virtue which made the novitiate tolerable
for him, and enabled him easily to acquire the
important monastic virtue of strict obedience.
The "lowly Seraphim," as he was to call himself
later, was not one to misconstrue the meaning
of his visions.

On September 2, 1793, at the age of thirty-four,
Seraphim was ordained priest by Bishop Theo-
philus of Tambov. He served in this capacity
with great fervor, celebrating the Divine Liturgy
daily — a rare practice, especially in 18th century
Russia.

In 1794, following the death of Abbot Pakhomius, to whom he was deeply attached, the blessed
hieromonk[22] felt free to request permission to
withdraw to a deserted part of the forest. The new
Abbot, Father Isaiah, readily granted it. Thus,
at the age of thirty-five, on the eve of the Feast
of the Presentation of the All-Holy Virgin in the
Temple, exactly sixteen years after his arrival at
the monastery, St. Seraphim left. He took with
him Holy Scripture and his icon of the Virgin
of Compassion. As his hermitage, he chose a spot
about three and a half miles from the monastery,
on the shore of the Sarovka River. Here there

was a small, one-room hut, made of logs. It was
furnished only with the icon, a stove, a wooden
chopping block which served him as a chair, and
a sack of stones for a bed. He wore the same cas-
sock — a white tunic bound by a cord — year-
round, adding a heavy overcoat in winter. On
his feet he wore birch bark sandals (*lapti*) in
summer, and high boots in winter, and always
he wore his black monastic cap.

His days were full. Adhering strictly to the rule
of prayer of St. Pachomios, prescribed for the
Desert Fathers, St. Seraphim arose about midnight
and recited the Midnight Service[23] and the Orthros, and read the First Hour. Before ten in the
morning, he began reading the offices for the
Third, Sixth and Ninth Hours, and the subsequent Typical Psalms.[24] At the end of the after-
noon, he recited the Vespers and, after his evening
meal, the Prayers after Supper (*Apodipno*).[25]
Before retiring, he said the Prayers before Sleep.
In addition, he intoned the Psalms, at first as appointed by the Rule of St. Pachomios, later according to a sequence which he had worked out
for himself, and which he called "The Private
Rule of Seraphim."[26] He also read the Scriptures, especially the Gospels. At all other times,

he continuously repeated the hesychast silent Prayer of the Heart.

St. Seraphim named his new home "Mount Athos," and mentally transformed the dark forest neighboring his barren hut by fancifully giving Biblical names to its various parts: Nazareth, Bethlehem, Jerusalem, Mount Thabor, Golgotha. In this way, as he went about his daily work, gathering moss as fertilizer for his vegetable garden in summer or chopping wood in winter, he could relive these various stages in the life of Christ, intoning appropriate hymns, and occasionally reading relevant prayers or Scriptural passages from the copy of the Gospels, which he always carried with him.

In this northern "Holy Land," the Saint could meet directly with God's creation. He welcomed the mosquitoes that infested the forest swamps where he gathered the moss. They were a joy to him, he said, for "the passions are destroyed through suffering and afflictions." His friendship with the animals of the forest was a source of wonder to his fellow monks. According to Father Joseph — an eye-witness — rabbits, foxes, lynx, lizards, bears, even wolves would gather at midnight around the entrance to the hut, waiting for

St. Seraphim to finish his prayers and come out to feed them with bread, which he always seemed to have left over for them. Several persons told of a bear which would obey his orders and run errands for him, such as fetching honey when there was a visitor. These acts on the bear's part always delighted the Saint.

His diet consisted of vegetables, which he grew, and of bread which was brought from the monastery.

On Saturdays and on the eve of feast days, he went to the monastery to take part in the Vespers and the Orthros and in the morning Divine Liturgy. He did not himself celebrate the Liturgy, feeling that he was unworthy, but only partook of Holy Communion. In spring he would spend the first week of Great Lent at the monastery, joining the monks in prayer and abstaining from all food.

St. Seraphim still felt the need for this occasional corporate worship, just as he did and would continue to feel, except on unusual occasions, the need for reading. But later he reached the stage of wholly silent prayer. "Man," he said, "stands in need of the Holy Scriptures because he is not yet possessed of the Holy Spirit. . . . Once the Spirit shall have taken hold of him, he will

Asked by a novice in later years how he had found strength for this feat, he replied: "St. Symeon the Stylite remained standing on a column for forty-seven years; can my efforts compare with his exploit?" "But did you feel the help of Divine grace?" the novice continued. "My joy," St. Seraphim replied, "of course. No man alone has sufficient strength." After a moment, he added: "When there is tenderness in the heart, God is with us."

This stage in the spiritual ascent of the Saint was reached after a criminal interruption in his life of solitude. On September 9, 1804, three ruffians in search of buried treasure or money in any form attacked him. In their disappointment at finding that he had nothing, they beat him mercilessly and left him for dead. He could well have defended himself, for he was a powerful man and was set upon while chopping wood, axe in hand. But he did not resist. It was only after more than a day had passed that he found the strength to drag himself to the monastery, suffering from multiple injuries to his head, chest, ribs, and back. Because of the obvious emergency, doctors were called from the nearby town of Arzamas. However, St. Seraphim did not wish their aid. While the doctors discussed the possibilities and

methods of treatment, he fell into a semi-coma
and once again saw the Theotokos accompanied
by the Apostles Peter and John. "What is the
use of doctors?" she said. "He is of our family."
Eight days after the attack, a few hours after this
vision, he was able to get up and walk a little;
and for the first time since his arrival at the monastery he could take some nourishment. But it
was not until five months had passed that he was
well enough to return to his hermitage and to
begin his thousand nights and days of standing.
Although he recovered, he was never to be the
man he had been: the tall, athletic monk. Still in
his mid-forties, he returned to his "Distant Hermitage" permanently marked, his back injuried
so that he could not stand straight again, able to
walk only bent over, using the aid of a stick or
shovel. Yet when his attackers were found, the
holy father insisted that they be allowed to go
free. The unprovoked attack, and his refusal to
defend himself or to see the criminals punished,
have been considered a martyrdom, and the visible
disabilities resulting from the attack as a martyr's
stigmata. His permanently bent posture has been
taken as a living symbol of his humility.

In 1807, just as St. Seraphim had completed
his three years as a Stylite, the Abbot of the mon-

tery, and he expressed concern. In fact, St. Seraphim's health had deteriorated. His days as a
Stylite had badly weakened his legs, and the
walk to the monastery was now very difficult for
him. Using this a pretext, on May 1, 1810, Father
Niphont presented an ultimatum: either St. Seraphim was to attend services regularly on Sundays
and feast days, or, if his health did not permit
it, he was to return to live in the monastery. On
May 8, 1810, after a week of prayer, St. Seraphim
returned to the monastery, to its activity, noise,
and the bustle of pilgrims. He believed that obedience is more important for a monk than fasting
and prayer.

At the monastery, he continued to practice
silence, having succeeded in receiving permission
to close himself in his cell and to receive Holy
Communion there. His food was brought to him
once a day. He received it on his knees, without
a word, his face covered with a large width of
linen. In his cell, he occupied himself with prayer
and reading. Thus, he read the New Testament
from beginning to end every week. He went out
only at night, for short walks around the church
or to the cemetery, silent, his face invisible. The
furnishings of his cell were the same as those of

his Distant Hermitage, except for the addition
of a coffin, which he had carved with his own
hands from an oak tree. The two small windows
of the cell offered a view of a ravine. His heat
and his only light at night and during the dark
Russian winter came from the sacred lamp before
the icon of the All-Holy Virgin of Compassion.
His clothing consisted of a shapeless white sack-
cloth garment and the black monastic cap. On
his chest he hung, for mortification, a heavy iron
cross nine inches long. Asked later by a novice
why he wore no chains or hair shirt, he replied:
"To endure, in accordance with the Gospel, the
insults of those who offend by word and the
bruises of those who do so by deed — that is our
chains, that is our hair shirt."

Now he no longer had even the animals of the
forest as visitors. But he had company of another
kind: the constant presence, through her icon,
of the Theotokos — the Joy of joys, as he called
her — and angels, who appeared and conversed
with him.

In 1815, after he had lived five years in the
cell in the manner that has been described, St.
Seraphim reached the stage of theosis, of union
with God. Now his life of solitude was no longer

highest personage in the land, Alexander I.[28] Neither this event, nor his fame among others, both high and low, affected him. He remained humble as before. All who came to him he met with the same salutation: "Greetings, my joy, Christ is risen." He bowed to the ground before each, and offered him or her a piece of holy bread dipped in wine. His door, shut for so many years, was now open to all. And he listened to every individual with equal attentiveness. He counseled in practical as well as spiritual matters, and in terms suited to each, treating each as unique and taking each one's troubles into his heart.

St. Seraphim knew intuitively how to reach each person according to the individual character of that person, frequently anticipating what the latter had to say. When his friend Father Antony, Abbot of the Monastery of Vissokogorsk, marvelled at this ability, the Saint explained it by saying that he spoke not from his own will and understanding, but by listening to the Holy Spirit and letting Him speak through him. "They come to me," he said, "and see in me a servant of God; and I, lowly Seraphim, consider myself as His humble servant, and what God orders His servant I transmit. I consider the first thought that comes to my mind as sent by God. What I say is spoken without my knowing what goes on in the heart of the person I am talking to, but in the belief that it is God's will and that it is for his good." Thus, "having by his life of prayer and heroic asceticism achieved an intimate union with God, at the same time he became in a way very close to men."[29]

The same Father Antony once came to St. Seraphim to bid him farewell. He felt that he would be seeing his companions no longer; thinking that he was about to die, he had started making rounds to take leave of his friends. "You do not understand," the Starets told him. "You will be leaving your monastery, but you are not to die yet. Instead, you will be appointed to head a large and famous monastery elsewhere." Sometime later, Father Antony was indeed named by Metropolitan Philaret of Moscow to serve as acting head of the renowned Monastery of the Holy Trinity-St. Sergius in Zagorsk.

St. Seraphim also foretold the circumstances which would surround his own death, saying that a fire would alert the monks about it. Further, he foretold the circumstances that would surround the official recognition of him as a saint. Without specific explanation, he said: "There will be

him who troubles me." And when asked about
his poor clothing, he said: "Johosaphat prized
the cloak given to him by the hermit Varlaam
more than royal purple." He ate only once a day.
His food consisted of cabbage and oats. The bed
in his cell at the monastery was still a sack filled
with stones. Towards the end of his life, he took
to sleeping on his knees, his head on his hands
and his back to the wall. When overwhelmed
by too many visitors, he occasionally took refuge
for a few hours of solitude in his Distant Hermitage.

Although entrusted by the Theotokos with the
care of the miraculous fountain in 1825, on the
day that he started back to his Distant Hermitage, the Saint had already received the gift of
healing. In 1823, when he still lived in voluntary
confinement in his monastic cell, a young land-
owner, Michael Manturov, was brought to him
This man had lost the use of his legs. Medical
intervention had been unsuccessful. He came to
the monastic cell as a last resort. "Do you believe in God?" St. Seraphim asked him. "For
him who believes, my joy, everything is possible."
When the young man replied affirmatively, the
Saint took some oil from the sacred lamp before
the icon of the All-Holy Virgin and rubbed it

on Manturov's legs and feet. The young man immediately found that he could stand and walk. He threw himself at the Starets' feet to thank him. "No, no, my joy," St. Seraphim said, raising him. "Only God does this; you owe your cure to Him and to His Holy Mother." In gratitude for his healing Manturov gave away all his worldly goods.

The most famous healing of St. Seraphim, however, is that of Nicholas Motovilov, a young member of the nobility, who came to him on September 7, 1831, the eve of the Feast of the Nativity of the Theotokos. Motovilov was suffering from a form of rheumatism such that he had to be carried by four men. All medical attempts had failed. After two conversations with him, the Starets asked Motovilov, on September 9, if he believed in Christ and the Theotokos, and in Christ's power to heal. When Motovilov replied that he did, the Starets told him that he was already cured. Hesitatingly, the young man stood. And after a few moments of uncertainty, he walked. Motovilov himself recorded the event.

These healings, the crowds of pilgrims, up to a thousand in a single day — persons of all walks of life, speaking all kinds of dialects, and in all variety of dress, coming not only to the fountain for physical healing, but also to the monastery compound for counsel or to benefit spiritually by simply seeing or hearing the Starets — annoyed some of the monks. So did his ascetic habits. But of all St. Seraphim's actions the most annoying to these monks was, it seems, his founding and material support of a women's religious community. Their attitude, however, hardly deterred him. Rather, the convent became of increasing concern to him as time went on.

Many years earlier, in 1780, in the small village of Diveyevo, seven miles from Sarov, but in the neighboring province of Nizhni-Novgorod, a wealthy widow named Agatha Melgunova, later Mother Alexandra, built a church and received permission to set up a women's community. In 1789, on her deathbed, she begged Father Pakhomius, Abbot of the Monastery of Sarov, not to abandon her "orphan girls." On the death of Pakhomius, their spiritual care was passed on to St. Seraphim. It was not until 1823, however, that he first became active in his concern. In that year, he asked Michael Manturov, whom he had just recently healed, to stake out some land near the old church. A year later, a new community was born, one of "miller women," so-called because its members could support themselves by a mill, which the Starets caused to be built on the same land. It differed from the old convent next to it in that married women and widows were not accepted: only virgins could belong to it. The Abbess of this community was the All-Holy Virgin herself, for it was she, according to the Starets, who instructed him in matters pertaining to its organization. The first members were peasant women, poor, totally uneducated. Later, they were joined by some women of the local gentry. A church was completed in 1829, donated by Manturov, whose sister, Helen, had joined the sisterhood. The church was consecrated on August 6, 1829, the day of the Feast of the Transfiguration, by the Bishop of Nizhni-Novgorod.

Although St. Seraphim did not personally visit the community, it was wholly under his direction. He gave the sisters a simple rule of unquestioning obedience, simple prayer three times a day, regular attendance of the Divine Liturgy on Sundays, uninterrupted reading of the Psalter in church — done in turns by twelve sisters so designated — as prayer for the living and the dead, and work at the mill and in the fields. He also asked them to recite the Jesus Prayer, and to partake of Holy Communion as frequently as possible. Because of their hard work in the fields, he discouraged undue fasting, and suggested that they take bread along with them when they went out to work. Finally, he asked that a candle always be kept burning before the icon of our Lord in the church, and that a sacred lamp always be kept lit in front of the icon of the Theotokos in the crypt. St. Seraphim provided all the candles. He also donated bread, salt, and firewood.

The sisters of Diveyevo were deeply grateful and devoted to St. Seraphim for all the provisions he made for their spiritual and material welfare. The community which he directed was for them an oasis of peace that transfigured the brutal life of the poverty-sticken mining village. They cherished the beauty, tenderness, and love which he taught them to find in God's creation. And they recognized him as a person who, by his long spiritual ascent, had triumphed over the flesh and at times over natural law as well. There were many events remembered as miracles done for them, but among the greatest was an impersonal one actually witnessed by a group of sisters. "We were walking in a meadow," one of the sisters wrote. "The grass was green and very high. . . .

We turned and looked back and saw Father Seraphim walking more than two feet above the ground, not even touching the grass. Frightened, we began to weep and fell at his feet. 'My joys,' he said, 'tell no one about this while I live, but after my departure from you, then, please recount it.' "
A similar instance of levitation was witnessed by a young nobleman who was suffering from paralysis and had come to the Saint for help. Turning suddenly, he saw Father Seraphim at prayer, raised above the ground. Father Seraphim asked him, too, not to speak about the event until after his death.

In his care and respect for the simple women of the community of Diveyevo, the Starets paid tribute both to the All-Holy Virgin who had often appeared to him, cared for him physically, and been his spiritual guide, and to the role played by the many saintly women in the development of Christianity. He also paid tribute to the pious women of Russia, who throughout its history have been a major source of its spiritual strength. The first of these was Olga, the mother of St. Vladimir, who converted Russia to the Christian faith.

St. Seraphim's relationship to the Theotokos, which found such concrete expression on his side in his care for the "orphans" of Diveyevo, who regarded her as their Abbess, is quite striking on her side as well. She had healed him three times. She had then given him the gift of healing others. She had been constantly with him in the icon of the Theotokos of Compassion, from his first years at the monastery. She had appeared to him and been his spiritual guide. In 1831, she appeared to him for the twelfth and last time. On March 24, the eve of the Feast of the Annunciation, St. Seraphim asked one of the sisters, Eupraxia (in the world Eudoxia Ephraimovna) to come to his cell at the monastery. She was afflicted in soul, because she was encountering difficulties in her life of spiritual endeavor, and the Starets wanted her to share in the spiritual joy of the vision of the Theotokos which it had been intimated to him that he would have. Together, they prayed through the night. At dawn, Eupraxia recounts, she heard a sound like that of wind rising in the forest and as it came closer singing swelled from it. St. Seraphim said to her: "Do not be afraid. Behold the Lord's grace coming down to us." The air was now scented as with the richest incense. Then she saw the Saint raise his arms and prostrate himself, crying out: "O, most holy Theotokos!" She saw two angels enter, preceding the entrance of the Queen of Heaven. On either side of the All-Holy Virgin were the Apostles John and Peter, and with them came twelve virgin martyrs, each with a crown. The cell was lit as with the blaze of a thousand candles, and the light continued to increase. Eupraxia was dazzled by the light and fell to the ground in a faint. The Theotokos herself raised her, presented the holy martyrs to her, and then turned to speak with St. Seraphim. Of their conversation Eupraxia could later remember only the last words of the Theotokos: "Soon, my dear one, you shall be with us." The vision lasted four hours.

St. Seraphim now began to make ready for his approaching death. He went to bid farewell to some, sent messages to others, and spoke a last goodbye to numerous visitors. He asked that he be laid in the coffin he had made and had so long had with him, and that the icon of the All-Holy Virgin appearing to St. Sergius be placed on his chest. He selected his place of burial, by the Church of the Dormition, the main church of the monastery. "In body," he told people, "I already feel dead to all, but in spirit I feel as strong as if I were newly born." With these words

his face would glow with the joyous light for
which he was renowned, and of which the most
famous account is given by Motovilov.[32]

The main concern of the divine Father these
last days continued to be for the sisters of Diveyevo, his "orphan girls," for whom he unerringly
foresaw troubled times, and whom he warned
with increasing emphasis to be patient and stead-
fast. He entrusted the community's earthly care
to Nicholas Motovilov. To all, but especially to
these sisters, he offered spiritual aid even after
his death. He told them: "When I am no longer,
come to my grave. Whenever you have time,
come, the more often the better. Gather up all
that is heavy on your heart, collect all that has
befallen you, and bring all your troubles to my
grave. Pressing yourself against the ground, tell
it all, as you would to one alive, and I shall hear
you and dissolve your sorrow. Speak to me as
you spoke to me while I lived. For to you I am
and shall be alive unto all ages. . . . I entrust you
to God and to our All-Holy Virgin. Have no
fear. After many trials, order will be restored to
the convent with the twelfth Mother Superior,
whose name will be Mary."

The prophecy was fulfilled. Trouble had already started during the Saint's lifetime, owing to the petty jealousy, narrow-mindedness, and even intrigue of some of the monks. The latter argued that his admitting nuns to his cell was causing scandal. Father Niphont attempted, by means of soldiers from the nearby garrison, to prevent the sisters from visiting the Starets. The whole community at Sarov resented the fact that he provided his "orphans" with communally owned fuel and food, as well as with much that pilgrims gave directly to him. The greatest threat, however, came from Ivan Tikhonovich (later Father Joasaph), an ambitious young monk, whom St. Seraphim had himself introduced into the women's community. This monk had been a disciple of his, but had little appreciation for what the Starets taught him. He wished to get control of the community and see it run his own way — a way that simply showed no understanding of the sisterhood's purpose. When the Saint was still living, Tikhonovich had the community investigated for scandal and illegality, charging that it lacked official status and harbored runaway serfs. The investigation, by both religious and civil authorities, found nothing out of order, and granted the community legal status. But Tikhonovich's intrigues did not stop, and for many years after the

Saint's death constituted a veritable persecution
of the sisterhood. Nevertheless, in 1862, after the
tonsure of its twelfth Mother Superior, Elizabeth
Ushakov, as a nun under the name of Mary, it was
raised to the rank of a convent, and peace was
finally restored.[33]

The holy Father, always casual about the many
candles he burned, would leave them burning
in his cell when he left for his forest retreat.
He assured the monks that there was no danger.
On the other hand, he said that his death would
be announced by a fire, as we have already noted.
On Sunday, January 1, 1833, the Starets came to
the Church of Saints Zosima and Savvas which
he had built in his youth in thanks for the cure of
his illness. He partook of the Holy Eucharist,
bowed with unusual veneration before the icons
of Christ crucified and of the Blessed Virgin on
the iconostasis, and bade farewell to his fellow
monks. His weakness was marked, but his attitude
was, as usual, one of quiet joy. He spent the day
receiving visitors. To a sister of Diveyevo he
gave two hundred roubles for bread, as a fulfill-
ment of his promise to care for his "orphans"
materially. He consoled the monks and novices,
saying: "Do not be dejected, be alert, the present

day prepares a crown." Three times he left his cell to meditate over the place he had designated for his grave. Late in the evening, he was heard intoning, not the expected hymns of the current Christmas season, but the hymns of Easter: "It is the Day of the Resurrection . . . ;" "Shine, Shine, O New Jerusalem . . . ;" and "Christ is risen from the dead. . . ."At about six o'clock the following morning, monks noticed smoke coming from his cell. When their knocks remained unanswered, they broke in and found a smouldering fire, started by a candle which had fallen from the Saint's hand. The Starets was kneeling before the icon of the All-Holy Virgin of Compassion, the "Joy of all joys," and had in front of him the Book of the Gospels, open. His hands were crossed on his chest, over the copper cross his mother had given him more than half a century earlier, when he left Kursk for the Monastery of Sarov. He seemed to have fallen asleep. Thus ended the earthly life of the holy Father.

St. Seraphim had said that there would one day be great joy in Sarov. "In the midst of summer," he had said, "there will be singing here in Sarov, singing as in the Paschal season, and people will flock here from all sides; yes, even the Emperor

himself." Seventy years after his death, on July
19, 1903, the 144th anniversary of his birth, the
Starets, who had long been recognized as a Saint
by the people, was officially recognized as a Saint
by the Church of Russia, in the presence of the
imperial family and of great multitudes of people
who had come to the Monastery of Sarov from
all parts of Russia.

Such was the life and character of St. Seraphim
of Sarov. He was a spiritual striver, a man of
prayer, a mystic who attained the goal of the
Christian life as he described it: the possession
of the grace of the Holy Spirit. He sought not
only his own good, but also the good of others,
having served as a teacher of monks, a protector
and spiritual guide of nuns, a healer and coun-
selor of an immense number of people. His life
as he lived it shone and continues to shine. It
guided those who came to him during his ministry
and countless others in the generations that followed, and serves as a great beacon in our own age.

A CONVERSATION WITH THE SAINT
BY NICHOLAS A. MOTOVILOV[1]

TRANSLATED BY MARY-BARBARA ZELDIN

It was a Thursday. The day was dark. Seven inches of snow lay on the ground and thick flakes were falling when Father Seraphim began his conversation with me. We were in a clearing close to his Near Hermitage, facing the Sarovka river, which flows at the foot of the hill. Father Seraphim seated me on the stump of a tree he had just felled, and squatted in front of me.

"The Lord has revealed to me," the great Starets said, "that in your childhood you were always wondering what was the goal of our Christian life, and that you repeatedly asked many famous religious and spiritual persons about it."

I must say here that from the age of twelve this matter had persistently bothered me, and that I had indeed approached many people of the clergy on this question, but their answers had not satisfied me. This, however, was unknown to the Starets.

"But no one," Father Seraphim continued, "gave you a precise answer. They said: 'Go to church, pray to God, live in accordance with God's commandments, do good — that, for you, is the goal of Christian life.' Some even grew angry with you on the grounds that your curiosity was displeasing to God, and they told you not to search into things that were beyond your grasp. But they did not speak as they ought. And so now I, lowly Seraphim, shall explain to you in what that goal really consists.

"Prayer, fasting, vigils, and all other Christian practices, however good they are in themselves, do not constitute the goal of our Christian life, although they serve as a necessary means to its attainment. *The true goal of our Christian life consists in the acquisition of the Holy Spirit of God.* Fasting, vigils, prayers, alms-giving and all good deeds done for the sake of Christ are but means for the acquisition of the Holy Spirit of God. But note, my son, that only a good deed done for the sake of Christ brings us the fruits of the Holy Spirit. All that is done, if it is not for Christ's sake, although it may be good, brings us no reward in the life to come, nor does it give us God's grace in the present life. This is why our Lord Jesus Christ said: 'He that gathereth not with Me, scattereth' (Luke 11:23) .[2] Not that a good deed can be called other than gathering, for although it is not done for Christ's sake, still it is good. The Scriptures say: 'In every nation, he that feareth God and worketh righteousness, is acceptable to Him' (Acts 10:35) . . . . "

"But what is 'acquiring?' " I asked Father Seraphim. "I don't really understand."

" 'Acquiring' is the same as 'gaining,' " he replied. "You understand, surely, what is meant by acquiring money? Acquiring the Holy Spirit of God is exactly the same thing. You understand, friend of God,[3] the meaning of acquiring in a worldly sense, don't you? The aim of the worldly life of ordinary people is the acquisition or making of money, and for nobles it is, in addition, the receiving of honors, marks of distinction and other rewards for government service. The acquisition of the Spirit of God is also capital, but a capital which dispenses grace and which is eternal. And

since it is very like monetary, social and temporal
capital, it is obtained in similar ways. God the
Logos, our Lord the God-Man Jesus Christ, com-
pares our life with the marketplace. He calls our
activity on earth trading, and says to us: 'Trade
till I come' (Luke 19:13), 'redeeming the time,
because the days are evil' (Eph. 5:16). In other
words, make the most of your time to obtain heavenly blessings through earthly goods. These
earthly goods are good works[4] done for Christ's
sake, conferring upon us the grace of the All-Holy
Spirit.

"In the parable of the wise and the foolish virgins, when the foolish ones ran out of oil they were
told: 'Go, buy it in the market.' But when they
had bought it the doors of the bridal chamber were
already shut and they were unable to enter. Some
say that the foolish virgins' lack of oil signifies lack
of good deeds in their lives. This interpretation is
not quite correct. Why should they lack good
deeds, when they are called virgins, even though
foolish ones? Virginity is one of the greatest virtues, comparable to an angelic state, and it could
replace all other virtues. I, lowly as I am, think
that in fact what they lacked was the grace of the
All-Holy Spirit of God. These virgins did good

works, but in their spiritual ignorance they supposed that the Christian life consisted only in doing good works. . . . They did not care whether they had thereby received the grace of the Spirit of God. . . . It is this acquisition of the Holy Spirit, symbolized by the oil, which the foolish virgins lacked. They were called foolish precisely because they had forgotten the essential fruit of virtue, the grace of the Holy Spirit, without which no one can be saved. . . . The Holy Spirit comes to dwell in our souls, and this indwelling of the Almighty in our souls, this abiding in our spirit of the Triadic Unity, is given to us only if we strive with all our strength to acquire the Holy Spirit. . . .

"The foolish virgins went to the market to buy oil when they saw that their lamps were going out, but they did not manage to return in time, and the door was already shut. The market is our life. The door of the nuptial chamber, closed and barring their way to the Bridegroom, is human death. The wise and the foolish virgins are Christian souls. The oil is not deeds, but the grace of the All-Holy Spirit of God which is received through deeds into our being, transforming corruption into incorruption, death of the soul into spiritual life, darkness into light, the cave of our being where the passions are enchained like cattle and wild beasts into a temple of God, into a shining bridal chamber of eternal joy in Jesus Christ our Lord, the Creator and Redeemer and Eternal Bridegroom of our souls.

"Of course, every good work done for the sake of Christ gives us the grace of the Holy Spirit, but prayer provides it most of all, for prayer is, as it were, always at hand as an instrument for the acquisition of the grace of the Spirit. For instance, you would like to go to church, but either there is no church or the service is over. Or, you would like to give alms to a beggar, but there is no beggar or you have nothing to give. Or, you would like to preserve your virginity, but you have not the strength, either because of your constitution, or because of the violence of the machinations of the enemy which you cannot withstand on account of your human weakness. Or, you would like to do some good deed or other for Christ's sake, but you have not the strength or the occasion does not arise. But nothing stands in the way of prayer: it is always possible for everyone, rich and poor, noble and lowly, strong and weak, healthy and sick, righteous and sinful. . . .

"Great is the power of prayer. More than anything else, it brings with it the Spirit of God, and its practice is available to everyone. . . .

"Truly, in prayer we are vouchsafed to converse with Him, our All-Gracious and Life-Giving God and Savior Himself. But even so we must pray only until the Holy Spirit of God descends upon us, granting us, to an extent known to Him alone, a measure of His heavenly grace. When He deigns to visit us we must stop praying. Why should we pray to Him: 'Come and dwell within us. Purify us from every blemish, and save our souls, O Gracious God?'[5] He has already come to us to save us. He has come to us who set our hope in Him and truly call on His holy name so that, hungering and thirsting for His coming, we may humbly and lovingly receive Him, the Comforter, into the temple of our souls.

"Let me clarify this for you with an example, friend of God. Suppose you have invited me as a guest to your home, and I have arrived at your house at your request and wish to converse with you, and you nevertheless continue to invite me, saying: 'Please come in, do come in.' Then I would have to say: 'What's the matter with him? Has he gone out of his mind? I have come to him and still he keeps calling for me.' So it is with our

Lord God the Holy Spirit. This is why it is said:
'Be still, and know that I am God; I will be exalted among the nations, I will be exalted in the
earth' (Ps. 45:11). That is, I shall appear and
shall continue to appear to everyone who believes
in Me and calls upon Me, and I shall converse with
him as I once conversed with Adam in Paradise,
with Abraham and Jacob and others of my servants, with Moses, Job, and those like them.

"Many think that this stillness is to be understood as having reference only to worldly matters — that is, that in conversing with God in
prayer we should be still to all worldly considerations. But I tell you, in the name of God, that although it is necessary to be still to these in prayer,
nevertheless, when by the all-powerful strength of
faith and prayer our Lord God, the Holy Spirit,
condescends to visit us and comes to us in the fullness of His ineffable goodness, we must be still
even to prayer. The soul speaks and converses in
prayer, but at the descent of the Holy Spirit one
should be completely silent, in order to hear clearly
and with full understanding all the words of eternal life which He will then deign to bring to us.
Moreover, the soul and spirit must be in a state
of extreme sobriety, and the body in a state of

chaste purity. . . ."

"Yes, Father, but what about other good deeds done for Christ's sake in order to acquire the grace of the Holy Spirit? You speak only of prayer."

"Acquire the grace of the Holy Spirit also by practicing all the other virtues for Christ's sake. Trade in them spiritually, trade with those of them which give you the greatest profit. . . . For instance, if prayers and vigils give you more of God's grace, keep vigil and pray; if fasting gives you much of the Spirit of God, then fast; if giving alms gives you more, then give alms. Weigh every good deed done for Christ's sake in this manner. . . .

"If we properly understand the commandments of Christ and of the Apostles, then we see that our enterprise as Christians does not consist in increasing the number of our good deeds, for they are merely means to our goal of a Christian life, but in deriving the utmost profit from them, that is, in acquiring the most abundant gifts of the Holy Spirit. . . ."

"Father," I said, "you keep on talking about the acquisition of the grace of the Holy Spirit as the aim of Christian life; but how and where can I see it? Good deeds are visible, but can the Holy Spirit be seen? How shall I know whether He is with me or not?"

"At the present time," the Starets replied, "because of the almost universal lukewarm attitude to holy faith in our Lord Jesus Christ, and because of lack of attention to the working within us of His Divine Providence and to the communion of man with God, we have reached such a point that one may say we are at a very great distance from true Christian life. The words of Holy Scripture, such as when the Spirit of God says through the mouth of Moses: 'And Adam saw the Lord walking in Paradise' (cf. Gen. 3:9), now seem strange to us. . . . Many other passages of Holy Scripture speak of God's appearing to men. That is why some people say: 'These passages are incomprehensible. Is it really possible for people to see God so manifestly?' But there is nothing incomprehensible here. This incomprehensibility has come about because we have strayed from the simplicity of original Christian knowledge. Under the pretext of enlightenment, we have reached such darkness of ignorance that by now the idea of God's appearing among people is inconceivable for us.

The ancients, on the other hand, understood it so clearly that it did not seem odd to them, even in ordinary conversation. Thus Job, when his friends rebuked him for blaspheming against God, replied to them: 'How can that be when I feel the breath of the Almighty in my nostrils?' (cf. Job 27:3). That is to say: 'How can I blaspheme against God when the Holy Spirit abides with me? If I were blaspheming against God, then the Holy Spirit would leave me; but, behold, I feel His breath in my nostrils.' In just the same way it is said of Abraham and Jacob that they saw God and conversed with Him, and Jacob even wrestled with Him. Moses and all the people with him saw God when it was granted to him to receive the tablets of the Law on Mt. Sinai. A pillar of cloud and a pillar of fire, that is, the evident grace of the Holy Spirit, served as guides to the people of God in the wilderness. People saw God and the grace of His Holy Spirit not in sleep or in dreams or in the delirium of deranged imagination, but actually revealed. . . .

"But when, by tasting from the tree of the knowledge of good and evil — prematurely and against the commandment of God — Adam and Eve learned the difference between good and evil

and fell subject to all the afflictions which followed
upon this transgression of God's commandment,
then they lost this priceless gift of the grace of the
Spirit of God. Thus, up to the coming of the God-
Man Jesus Christ into the world, the Spirit of God
was not in the world, 'because Jesus was not yet
glorified' (John 7:39). However, this does not
mean that the Spirit of God had wholly abandoned
the world, but His presence there was not so complete as in Adam or in us Orthodox Christians. He
appeared only externally, although the signs of
His presence in the world were known to mankind.
Thus, for example, many mysteries concerning the
future salvation of mankind were revealed to
Adam, and to Eve as well, after the Fall. And for
Cain, in spite of his impiety and transgression, it
was easy to understand the Divine grace-giving
voice conversing with him even though it de-
nounced him. Noah conversed with God. Abraham saw God and His day and rejoiced. The grace
of the Holy Spirit acting externally was also re-
flected in all the Old Testament prophets and
saints of Israel. . . .

"The presence of the Spirit of God also acted
among pagans who did not know the true God,
although it did so less strongly than among God's
people. Indeed, even among them God found for

Himself chosen people. Such, for instance, were the virgin prophetesses, the Sybils, who dedicated their virginity to an Unknown God, but still to God, the Creator of the universe, the Almighty, the Ruler of the world, as the pagans conceived Him. Such also were the pagan philosophers who, although they too wandered in the darkness of ignorance of the Deity, yet sought the truth which is beloved of God. By this very God-pleasing search they were enabled to partake of the Spirit of God. For it is said that the nations which are ignorant of God practise His commandments by nature, and by nature do what is pleasing to Him (cf. Rom. 2:14). The Lord so praises truth that He says of it through the Holy Spirit: 'Truth has sprung out of the earth; and righteousness hath looked down from heaven' (Ps. 84:12).

"So you see, friend of God, both among the holy Hebrew people, a people beloved of God,[6] and among the pagans who did not know God, there was preserved a knowledge of God, that is, my son, a clear and rational understanding of how our Lord God the Holy Spirit acts in man, and precisely by what outer and inner sensations one can make sure that this action is an action of our Lord God the Holy Spirit and not an enticement of the enemy. This is the way it was from the fall of Adam to the coming of our Lord Jesus Christ into the world in the flesh. . . .

"But when our Lord Jesus Christ condescended to complete the whole work of salvation, after His Resurrection He breathed on the Apostles, restored the breath of life lost by Adam, and granted them the same grace of the All-Holy Spirit of God which Adam had enjoyed. But that is not all. He also told the Apostles that it was better for them that He go to the Father, for if He did not go the Spirit of God would not come into the world; but if He, Christ, went to the Father, then He would send the Spirit into the world and He, the Comforter, would guide them and all who followed their teaching into all truth, and would remind them of all the things He had said to them while He was still with them in the world (cf. John 16:7, 16:13, 14:26). This was the grace He had already promised them, 'grace for grace' (John 1:16).

"And on the day of Pentecost, He formally sent down to them the Holy Spirit like a rushing mighty wind, in the form of tongues of fire. These alighted on each of them, and entered into them, and filled them with the fiery strength of Divine grace. . . . (Acts 2: 1-4). This same fire-infusing grace of the Holy Spirit, when it is given to us all, the faithful in Christ, in the Sacrament of Holy Baptism, is sealed by the Sacrament of Chrismation on the chief parts of our bodies, as decreed by the Holy Church, the eternal keeper of this grace. During Chrismation we say: 'The seal of the gift of the Holy Spirit.'[7] And on what, my son, friend of God, do we, lowly as we are, place our seals, if not on vessels which contain some very precious treasure? And what in the world can be higher and more precious than the gift of the Holy Spirit sent down to us from on high in the Sacrament of Baptism? This grace of Baptism is so great and indispensible, so vital for man, that it is not taken away even from a heretic until his death. That is, it is not taken from him until the end of the period appointed on high by God's providence as a lifelong test of man on earth — a test to see what a man can accomplish by means of the strength of grace given to him from on high in the time allotted to him by God.

"If we did not sin we would remain forever saints of God, pure and free from all pollution of body and spirit. But the trouble is that as we grow in age we do not grow in grace or in the knowledge of God, but, on the contrary, little by little we

become corrupt and lose the grace of the Holy
Spirit of God, and in various degrees become
sinners, even very sinful people. But the wisdom
of God [ever] seeks our salvation and embraces
all things. And when a man resolves for its sake to
devote the early hours of the morning to God, and
to be watchful for the sake of his eternal salvation,
then, obeying its voice, he must hasten to offer
true repentence for all his sins, and to practice the
virtues contrary to the sins he has committed.
Then, through the virtues practiced for Christ's
sake, he will acquire the Holy Spirit, Who acts in
us and establishes in us the Kingdom of God. . . .

"In spite of men's fall into sin, in spite of the
darkness surrounding our souls, the grace of the
Holy Spirit granted at Baptism in the name of the
Father, and of the Son, and of the Holy Spirit,
shines in men's hearts with the Divine light which
has been, from time immemorial, the light of the
priceless gifts of Christ. If a sinner does not re-
pent, this light of Christ cries to the Father:
'Abba, Father, do not harden your heart forever
against this sinner.' And then, at the sinner's con-
version to the way of repentance, it completely
erases all traces of the sins that were committed,
and clothes the former sinner afresh with a robe

of incorruptibility, woven from the grace of the
Holy Spirit, about whose acquisition I have been
talking to you, friend of God, for such a long time
as the goal of Christian life.

"Still, so that you may understand even more
clearly, I must tell you what is meant by the grace
of God, how to recognize it, and how its activity
particularly manifests itself in the people whom
it enlightens. The grace of the Holy Spirit is the
light which enlightens man. All Holy Scripture
speaks of this. Thus David, the Forefather of
[Christ] God, said: "Thy Law is a lamp unto my
feet, and a light unto my paths' (Ps. 118: 105),
and 'Were it not that Thy Law is my meditation,
then I should have perished in mine afflliction'
(Ps. 118: 92). That is to say: The grace of the
Holy Spirit which is expressed in the Law by the
words of the Lord's commandments is my lamp
and my light. If this grace of the Holy Spirit (for
which I so painstakingly and diligently strive, that
seven times a day I meditate upon the righteousness of Thy judgments) did not enlighten me in
the darkness of the cares inherent in the high calling of my royal rank, whence could I receive a
spark of light to lighten my way along the road of
life, darkened as it is by the ill-will of my enemies?

"And, indeed, the Lord has often demonstrated before many witnesses how the grace of the Holy Spirit operates with regard to those people whom He has sanctified and illumined by His great visitation. Remember Moses after his conversation with God on Mount Sinai. He shone with such an extraordinary light that people could not look at him, and he had to cover his face; he could not even appear in public without covering it with a veil. Remember the Transfiguration of the Lord on Mount Thabor. A great light surrounded Him and 'His garments became shining, exceedingly white like snow' (Mark 9: 2), and His disciples fell on their faces from fear. In the same way the grace of the Holy Spirit of God manifests itself in an ineffable light to all to whom God reveals its activity."

"But how," I asked Father Seraphim, "can I know that I am in the grace of the Holy Spirit?"

This is very simple, friend of God," he answered. "That is why the Lord says: 'All things are evident to those that understand' (Prov. 8: 9). The trouble is that we do not seek this divine understanding, which is not presumptuous, because it is not of this world. This understanding, which is full of love for God and for our neighbor, fashions every man for his salvation. Of this understanding the Lord said: God 'desires all men to be saved, and to come unto the knowledge of truth' (1 Tim. 2: 4). And of the lack of this understanding He said to His Apostles: 'Are ye also yet without understanding?' (Matt. 15: 16). Concerning this understanding it is said of the Apostles in the Gospel: The Lord 'opened their understanding, that they might understand the Scriptures' (Luke 24:45). Once they had received this understanding, the Apostles always perceived whether or not the Spirit of God abode with them. And filled with the Spirit of God and perceiving His presence in them, they affirmed that their work was holy and entirely pleasing to the Lord God. This explains why they wrote in their Epistles: 'It seemed good to the Holy Spirit and to us' (Acts 15:28). Only on these grounds did the Holy Apostles, palpably conscious of the presence of the Spirit of God within them, offer their Epistles as truth. And so, friend of God, do you see how simple this is?"

"Still," I replied, "I do not understand how I can be fully certain of being in the Spirit of God. How can I myself discern His true presence within me?"

"I have already told you, friend of God," Father Seraphim replied, "that it is very simple, and I have explained to you in detail how people come to be in the Spirit of God, and how His presence within us should be known. What more do you need, my son?"

"I need," I said, "to understand this completely."

Father Seraphim then took me very firmly by the shoulders and said: "We are both, you and I, in the Spirit of God at this moment, my son. Why do you not look at me?"

"I cannot look, Father," I replied, "because great flashes of lightning are springing from your eyes. Your face shines with more light than the sun, and my eyes ache from the pain."

"Don't be frightened, friend of God," Father Seraphim said. "You yourself have now become as bright as I am. You are now yourself in the fullness of the Spirit of God: otherwise you would not be able to see me like this."

Then, bending his head towards me, he said softly in my ear: "Thank the Lord God for His

ineffable mercy towards you. You saw that I did
not even cross myself; I merely prayed to the Lord
God in thought in my heart and said within myself: 'Lord, grant him that he may see clearly with
the eyes of the flesh that descent of Thy Spirit
which Thou grantest to Thy servants when Thou
art pleased to appear in the light of Thy majestic
glory.' And behold, my son, the Lord immediately
fulfilled the humble request of lowly Serphim.
How then shall we not thank Him for this ineffable gift to us both? My son, the Lord God does
not always show His mercy in this way even to
great hermits. This grace of God has been pleased
to comfort your contrite heart, caring for you like
a loving mother, through the intercession of the
Mother of God herself. But why don't you look at
me, my son? Just look and don't be afraid! The
Lord is with us!"

At these words, I looked at his face and was
seized with an even greater sense of trembling
awe. Imagine in the center of the sun, in the most
dazzling brilliance of its noontime rays, the face
of a man talking to you. You see the movement of
his lips, the changing expression of his eyes, you
hear his voice, you feel that someone is holding
his hands on your shoulders. Yet you do not see
his hands or his body, but only a blinding light

spreading around for several yards, illumining with its brilliant sheen both the bank of snow covering the glade and the snow flakes that fall on me and on the great Starets. Can you imagine the state I was in?

"How do you feel now?" Father Seraphim asked me.

"Extraordinary well," I said.

"How 'well?' How exactly do you feel?"

"I feel," I replied, "such quiet and peace in my soul that I have no words to express them."

"This, friend of God," said Father Seraphim, "is that peace of which the Lord spoke to His disciples, saying: 'My peace I give unto you: not as the world giveth, give I unto you' (John 14:27). . . . For, to those whom the world hates but whom the Lord has chosen the Lord gives that peace which you now feel within you, the peace which, in the words of the Apostle, 'surpasseth all understanding' (Philip. 4:7) . . . . And what else do you feel?" Father Seraphim asked me.

"An extraordinary sweetness."[8]

And he continued: "This is that sweetness of which it is said in Holy Scripture: 'They shall be inebriated with the plenty of Thy house; and Thou shalt cause them to drink of the torrent of Thy delights' (Ps. 35:8). . . . And what else do you feel?"

"An extraordinary joy in all my heart."

And Father Seraphim continued: "When the Spirit of God comes down to a man and casts over him the fullness of His visitation, then the human soul is filled with an ineffable joy, for the Spirit of God creates joy in all that He touches. . . . This is that same joy of which the Lord speaks in His Gospel: 'A woman, when she is in labor, hath sorrow, because her hour is come; but when she hath brought forth the child, she remembereth no more the anguish, for joy that a man is born into the world' (John 16:21). 'In the world ye will have sorrow, but when I see again, your heart shall rejoice; and your joy no man shall take from you' (John 16:33, 22). But however comforting this joy which you now feel in your heart may be, it cannot compare with that joy of which the Lord Himself spoke through the mouth of His Apostle: 'Eye hath not seen, nor ear heard, neither have entered into the heart of man, the things which God hath prepared for them that love Him' (1 Cor. 2:9) . A foretaste of this joy is given to us now, and if it fills our souls with such sweetness, well-being and good cheer, then what can we say of that joy which is prepared in Heaven for those who sorrow here on earth? . . . What else do you feel, friend of God?"

"An extraordinary warmth," I replied.

"How can you feel warmth, my son? Look, we are in the forest, it is winter out here, there is snow under our feet and considerable snow on us, and snowflakes are still falling. What kind of warmth can this be?"

"The kind which there is in a bath-house," I replied, "when they pour water on the stone and steam rises in clouds."

"And the scent?" he asked me. "Is it the same as in a bath-house?"

"No," I replied. "Nothing on earth can compare with this fragrance. During my mother's lifetime, when I liked to dance and used to go to balls and evenings of dancing, my mother would spray me with perfume which she bought in the most fashionable shops of Kazan, but these perfumes had no such fragrance."

"My experience is just like yours, my son," Father Seraphim said with a friendly smile. "I am questioning you on purpose, to see whether you feel this in the same way. It is absolutely true, friend of God, no perfume on earth can compare with the pleasure of the heavenly fragrance we are now sensing, for what now envelops us is the fragrance of the Holy Spirit of God. What earthly thing could be like it? Note, friend of God, you told me we were surrounded with warmth, as in a bath-house; but, behold, the snow is not melting on you or me or beneath our feet. This warmth, then, is not in the air, but comes from within us. It is that very warmth of which the Holy Spirit makes us cry out to the Lord in prayer: 'Warm me with the warmth of Thy Holy Spirit.' Warmed by this warmth both men and women hermits had no fear of winter frosts, for they were clad as if with fur coats in the grace-given clothing woven by the Spirit of God. And this is how it should be in fact, because the grace of God ought to dwell within us, in our hearts, for the Lord said: 'The Kingdom of God is within you' (Luke 17:21). By the Kingdom of God the Lord meant the grace of the Holy Spirit. This Kingdom of God is now within you, and the grace of the Holy Spirit shines upon us and warms us from without as well, and, filling the air around us with many varied fragrances, it sweetens our senses with heavenly sweetness and floods our hearts with unutterable joy. Our present state is that of which the Apostle says: 'The Kingdom of God is not food and drink; but righteousness, and peace, and joy in the Holy Spirit' (Rom. 14:17). Our faith consists not in the plausible words of earthly wisdom, but in the evidence of the Spirit and of power (cf. 1 Cor. 2:4). This is the state in which we now find ourselves. Concerning this state the Lord said: 'There are some of them that stand here, who shall not taste of death, till they see the Kingdom of God come with power' (Mark 9:1). Behold, my son, you who love God, what ineffable joy the Lord God is now granting unto us! This is what is meant by being in the fullness of the Holy Spirit, what is meant by St. Macarios of Egypt when he writes: 'I myself was in the fullness of His Holy Spirit.' I think that from now on you shall no longer ask, friend of God, how the grace of the Holy Spirit manifests itself in men. Will you remember this manifestation of God's ineffable mercy that has been visited upon us?"

"I don't know, Father," I said, "whether the Lord will grant it to me to remember this mercy of God always as vividly and clearly as I sense it now."

"I believe," Father Seraphim answered me, "that the Lord will enable you to retain this in your memory forever; otherwise His goodness would not have immediately bowed to my humble prayer, and would not have been prepared so quickly to hear the petition of the lowly Seraphim. And this is all more the case since it is not given to you for you alone to understand, but through you for the whole world, so that you may yourself be confirmed in God's work and can be useful to others.

"As for the fact that I am a monk while you are a man in the world, that is quite beside the point. God demands true faith in Him and in His Only-Begotten Son. In return for this, He grants the grace of the Holy Spirit in abundance from on high. The Lord seeks a heart filled with love for God and for one's neighbor — this is the throne where He would sit and where He appears in the fullness of His heavenly glory. 'Son, give me thy heart' (Prov. 23:26), He says, 'and all the rest I will add unto thee' (cf. Matt. 6:33), for the human heart can contain the Kingdom of God. The Lord commanded His disciples: 'Seek ye . . . first the Kingdom of God, and His righteousness, and all these things shall be added unto you; for your heavenly Father knoweth that ye have need of all these things' (Matt. 6:33, 32) . . . . The Lord Jesus descended to us from heaven not to be served by men, but Himself to serve them and to give His life for the salvation of many. And so you, friend of God, do likewise and, now that God's mercy has visibly been manifested to you, tell of it to every man who desires his salvation. 'The harvest truly is plentiful,' the Lord says, 'but the laborers are few' (Matt. 9:37, Luke 10:2). The Lord God has led us out to work, and given us the gift of His grace, so that by reaping the grain of the salvation of our neighbors, and bringing them in large numbers into the Kingdom of God, we may bring Him fruit — some thirty-fold, some sixty-fold, some one hundred-fold. . . .

"And so, friend of God, all that you may ask of the Lord God you shall receive, provided only that it is for the glory of God or for the good of your neighbor. For He ascribes the good of our neighbor to His own glory, and that is why He says: 'All that you do unto the least of these, you do unto Me' (cf. Matt. 25:40). So have no doubt that the Lord God will fulfill your petitions, provided only that they be concerned with the glory of God or the good and edification of your neighbor. But even if it is something for your own need, use or advantage, the Lord God will be pleased to send you even that, just as quickly and graciously, provided it is a thing of extreme and indispensible need, for the Lord loves those that love Him. The Lord is good to all men, He gives in abundance to those who call on His name, and His bounty is in all His works. 'He will do the desire of them that fear Him, and He will hear their prayer' (Ps. 144:19), and realize all their intentions. . . .

"And so, friend of God, I have now told you and demonstrated to you all that the Lord and His All-Holy Mother have been pleased to tell you and show you through me, lowly Seraphim. Now go in peace. The Lord and the Mother of God be with you always, both now and unto the ages of ages. Amen."

During all this conversation, from the time when the face of Father Seraphim became illuminated, this vision continued. And all that he told me from the beginning of the narrative up to now he told remaining in one and the same position. The ineffable brilliance of the light which emanated from him I myself saw with my own eyes, and I am ready to confirm it on oath.

SPIRITUAL COUNSELS OF THE SAINT[1]

Translated by Mary-Barbara Zeldin

1. *On God*

God is a fire that warms and kindles the heart
and inward parts. Hence, if we feel in our hearts
the cold which comes from the devil — for the
devil is cold — let us call on the Lord. He will
come to warm our hearts with perfect love, not
only for Him but also for our neighbor, and the
cold of him who hates the good will flee before
the heat of His countenance.

2. *On Hope*

All who have firm hope in God are raised to
Him and illumined by the radiance of the eternal
light. If a man does not let excessive concern for
himself turn him away from love for God and for
acts of virtue, then this hope is true and wise. But
if a man places all his hope in his own affairs and

turns to God with prayer only when unforeseen misfortunes befall him, and seeing no means in his own powers to avert them begins to rely on the help of God, his hope is vain and deceptive. True hope seeks first of all the Kingdom of God, and is confident that every earthly necessity of temporal life will doubtless be given. . . . The heart can have no peace so long as it does not acquire such hope. . . . It is of this hope that our Savior's most holy words speak to us: "Come unto me, all ye that labor and are burdened, and I shall give you rest" (Matt. 11:28); that is, hope in Me and you shall be comforted in your labor and cares.

3. *On Love for God*

He who has achieved perfect love exists in this world as though he does not exist in it, for he considers himself a stranger to what is visible, and patiently awaits the invisible. He is wholly turned away from it towards love for God and forgetful of every other love. . . . The soul, full of love for God, then leaves the body; it has no fear of the unsubstantial power of this world, but flies off with angels as though from a foreign land to a land of its own.

4. *On the Preservation of Truths One has Come to Know*

One should not open one's heart to another unnecessarily. Out of a thousand you will find only one that will preserve your secret.

With a person of this world one must speak of worldly things, but with a man whose mind is of a spiritual nature one must speak of heavenly things.

5. *On Talkativeness*

An attentive man need but talk a lot with such as are of a contrary disposition for his inner self to be thrown into confusion.

But the really deplorable thing is that this results in the extinguishing of the fire which our Lord Jesus Christ came to re-establish in our hearts. For nothing so weakens the fire kindled in the heart of a monk by the Holy Spirit for the sanctification of his soul as communication and talk and chatter, excepting conversations with those who are sons of the divine mysteries, conversations for the restoration of the mind and for spiritual fellowship. (See Isaac of Syria, *Hom.* 5) .

6. *On Prayer*

A man who has decided to serve the Lord God must practice awareness of God and uninterrupted prayer to Jesus Christ, mentally repeating: "Lord Jesus Christ, Son of God, have mercy upon me, a sinner." After dinner one can say this prayer: "Lord Jesus Christ, Son of God, through the prayers of the Theotokos, have mercy upon me, a sinner;" or resort directly to the Most Holy Theotokos, praying: "Most Holy Theotokos, save us;" or repeat the angelic greeting: "Rejoice, O Virgin Theotokos." With such exercise, with preservation from distraction and with the maintainance of peace of mind, it is possible to come to God and become one with Him. For, according to the words of Isaac the Syrian, we cannot come near to God without uninterrupted prayer *(Hom.* 69).

St. John Chrysostom well described the virtue of prayer. Prayer, he said, is a mighty weapon, an unlimited treasure, independent wealth, a quiet haven, a reservoir of silence; it is the root and the source and the mother of ten thousand blessings *(Hom. on Inscrutability,* 5).

If in prayer it happens that the mind is caught up by distracting thoughts, then one should bow down to our Lord God and ask for forgiveness, saying: I have sinned, O Lord, in word, deed and thought, and all my senses.

One must always strive against giving in to mental distractions. Through these the soul is turned away from the consciousness of God and His love to the activity of the devil. As St. Macarios says: "All the eagerness of our enemy is to turn our thought away from remembrance of God and of fear and love of Him" (*Hom.* 2, Ch. 15).

When the mind and the heart are united in prayer, and nothing disturbs the soul's contemplation, then the heart is warmed with spiritual heat and the light of Christ operates, filling the whole inner man with peace and joy.

7. *On Sorrow*

A soul filled with sorrow, made mindless and frenzied, cannot either accept good advice or answer proffered questions with gentleness. . . . Whoever masters passions masters sorrow as well.

He who loves the world cannot but sorrow, whereas he who has turned away from the world is eternally joyous.

As fire purifies gold, so sorrow that is in accord with God purifies a sinful heart.

8. *On Despondency*

Just as the Lord cares for our salvation, so the
the devil, the killer of men, strives to lead man to
despondency.

When despondency seizes us, let us not give in
to it. Rather, fortified and protected by the light
of faith, let us with great courage say to the spirit
of evil: "What are you to us, you who are cut off
from God, a fugitive from Heaven, and a slave of
evil? You dare not do anything to us: Christ, the
Son of God, has dominion over us and over all.
Leave us, you thing of bane. We are made stead-
fast by the uprightness of His Cross. Serpent, we
trample on your head."

9. *On Patience and Humility*

One should always endure all things with gratitude, for God's sake.

Our life is but a minute in comparison with
eternity. Therefore, according to the Apostle, "the
sufferings of this present time are not worthy to be
compared with the glory to come which shall be
revealed in us" (Rom. 8:18) .

When someone disparages and abuses you, try

as far as possible to forgive him, in accordance with the Gospel: "Of him that taketh away thy goods ask them not again" (Luke 6:30).

When people revile us, we should consider ourselves unworthy of praise. If we were worthy, all would defer to us.

We should always and foremost humble ourselves, following the teaching of St. Isaac of Syria: "Humble yourself and you will behold the glory of God."

Therefore let us love humility, and we shall behold the glory of God. His glory is imparted to us in proportion as we become humble.

If there were no light all things would be dark. Similarly, without humility there is nothing in man but darkness.

10. *On Care of the Soul*

We should have every concern for our soul, and should strengthen our body for this reason only, that it may assist in the strengthening of the soul.

Voluntarily to exhaust our body to the point that the spirit is exhausted is an unreasonable mortication, even if it is done to acquire virtue.

11. *On Provision of the Soul*

The soul must be provided with the word of God, for the word of God, as Gregory the Theologian tells us, is the bread of angels of which souls partake that hunger after God. Most importantly, one must practice reading the New Testament and the Psalter. By so doing the mind is enlightened and undergoes a divine change.

One should so train himself in this that the mind swims, as it were, in the Law of the Lord, the Law which must guide and direct our lives.

It is very useful to spend time reading the word of God in solitude and to read the whole Bible with understanding. In return for this exercise alone, without the addition of any other virtuous deeds, the Lord grants man His mercy and fills him with the gift of understanding.

When a man provides his soul with the word of God, then he is granted the understanding of what is good and what is evil.

The reading of the word of God must be done in solutude, so that the whole mind of the reader may be immersed in the truths of the Holy Scriptures and may receive from them that heat which in solitude produces tears. Through these the whole man is warmed and filled with spiritual gifts, which delight the mind and heart beyond all words. One should also provide the soul with knowledge of the Church, how it has been preserved from the beginning to the present, and what it has suffered in this or that time.

One should know these things, not in order to lord over men, but in case he should encounter some powerful opposition. But most of all it should be done for oneself, in order to acquire peace of soul, in accordance with the teaching of the Psalmist: "Much peace have they that love Thy Law" (Ps. 118:165).

12. *On Peace of the Soul*

Nothing is better than peace in Christ, which repulses all the attacks of the evil spirits of the air and of the earth: "For our wrestling is not against flesh and blood, but against principalities, against powers, against the rulers of the darkness of this world, against the spirits of wickedness in the heavenly places" (Eph. 6:12).

It is a sign of an understanding soul if a man mentally looks within himself and has activity in his heart. Then the grace of God dawns in him, and he is in a state of peace, and so in a state out of this world, because his mind contemplates within himself the grace of the Holy Spirit, in accordance with the words of God: "His place is in peace" (Ps. 75:2).

Can we not rejoice when we see the sun with the eyes of the flesh? But how much greater is the joy when, with the inner eye, the mind sees Christ, the Sun of Righteousness. Then verily we rejoice with the joy of angels. Of this the Apostle said: "Our conversation is in Heaven" (Phil. 3:20).

When a man walks in the ways of peace, he picks up the gifts of the Spirit as it were with a spoon. . . . When a man attains a state of peace, he can shed on others the light of an enlightened understanding. But first he must repeat to himself the prophetic words: "Thou hypocrite, first cast out the beam out of thine own eye, and then shalt thou see clearly to cast out the mote out of thy brother's eye" (Matt. 7:5).

This peace, our Lord Jesus Christ left like a priceless treasure to His disciples before His death, saying: "Peace I leave with you, my peace I give unto you" (John 14:27). The Apostle also speaks of it: "And the peace of God, which passeth all understanding, shall keep your hearts and minds in Christ Jesus" (Phil. 4:7).

Hence we must concentrate all our thoughts, all our desires, and all our actions to this end, that we ever call out with the Church: "O Lord our God, grant us peace."

13. *On the Preservation of the Peace of the Soul*

One should in all ways endeavor to preserve the peace of the soul and not be troubled by the insults of others. For this a man must endeavor in every way possible to restrain anger and hold the mind and heart fast from any unfitting movement. . . .

For the preservation of the peace of the soul a man must also avoid condemning others. By not condemning others, and by keeping silent, the peace of the soul is preserved. When a man is in such a frame of mind he receives Divine revelations.

In order to get rid of [the habit of] condemning others, one must turn his attention to himself and not accept alien thoughts, but rather be dead to everything external.

14. *On Guarding the Heart*

We must indefatigably guard our hearts from improper thoughts and impressions, in accordance with the saying: "Keep thy heart with all watchfulness, for out it are the issues of life" (Prov. 4:23) .

Constant watchfulness over our heart gives birth within it to the purity of which the Lord said, according to the assurance of Eternal Truth: "Blessed are the pure in heart, for they shall see God" (Matt. 5:8) .

We ought not to pour out unnecessarily the good that has flowed into our heart. For what has been gathered up can be secure from visible and invisible enemies only when it is preserved in the depths of the heart.

When there is living water heated by Divine fire in it, then the heart boils. But when the water is poured out the heart grows cold and a man freezes.

15. *On Recognizing the Movement of the Heart*[2]

When a man receives something Divine, his heart rejoices, but when it is something diabolical, it is troubled.

When it accepts a Divine gift, the heart of a Christian does not require external proof that this gift is from the Lord. Rather, the heart is persuaded by that very same Divine action that its perception has a heavenly source. For it feels in itself the fruits of the Spirit: "Love, joy, peace, longsuffering, benignity, goodness, faith, meekness, continence" (Gal. 5:22-23).

But even though the devil should transform himself into an angel of light (2 Cor. 11:14), or present thoughts which seem most good, the heart will feel a certain lack of clarity, an unrest in its thoughts and a confusion of feeling.

16. *On Ascetic Progress*

One must be patient with regard to the weaknesses and imperfections of his soul, and endure his own shortcomings as he endures those of others. However, he must not grow lazy, but must urge himself on to do better.

17. *On Fasting*

It is not suited to everyone to follow a severe rule of abstinence from everything, or to deprive himself of everything which can serve for the easing of weakness.

One should make use of food daily to the extent that the body, fortified, may be the friend and assistant of the soul in the practice of virtue. Otherwise, the soul may weaken because it is exhausted.

On Wednesdays and Fridays, especially during the four fasts, eat once a day, and the angel of the Lord will remain with you.

18. *On Solitude and Silence*

It is most important to adorn oneself with silence. St. Ambrose of Milan says: "I saw many saved by silence; not one by loquacity." Again, one of the Fathers says that silence is the sacrament of of the world to come, while speech is the tool of this world.

You need only stay in your cell in attentiveness and silence and try by every means to move nearer to the Lord, and the Lord will be prepared to make you from a man into an angel.

When we remain in silence the adversary, the devil, can do nothing to the recesses of the human heart. But it must be understood that this refers to the silence of discursive reason *(razum)*. To go through such an exploit, a man must place all his trust in the Lord God, in accordance with the Apostle: "Casting all your care upon Him; for He careth for you" (1 Pet. 5:7).

If it is not possible always to abide in solitude and silence when one lives in a monastery and attends to the tasks set by a superior, then, even though there is little time remaining after completing these tasks, that time should be devoted to solitude and silence. Even for this little the Lord God will not refrain from sending down His grace in abundance.

From solitude and silence are born mercy and gentleness. The action of the latter in the heart of man can be compared to that calm water of Siloam which flowed without noise or sound, as

the prophet Isaiah says: "the water of Siloam . . .
goes silently (Isa. 8:6) .

Absolute silence is a cross on which a man must
crucify himself with all his passions and lusts. But
consider our Master Christ, how much abuse and
how many insults He suffered, and then even took
on the Cross. So it is not permitted to us to ar-
rive at absolute silence and to hope for saintly
perfection if we do not suffer with Christ.

19. *On the Active and the Contemplative Life*

The contemplative life must be approached
with fear and trembling, with a humble and a
contrite heart, after much probing of Holy Scripture and if possible under the direction of an experienced Starets, not with audacity or on one's
own authority.

If a guide capable of leading one in the con-
plative life cannot be found, then a man must be
guided by the Holy Scriptures. For the Lord Himself enjoins us to learn from the Holy Scriptures,
saying: "Search the Scriptures, for in them ye think
ye have life everlasting" (John 5:39) .

The way of the active life consists in fasting,

abstinence, vigils, prostrations, and other bodily practices, which constitute the narrow and painful way that leads, according to the saying of God, to life eternal (Matt. 7:14).

The way of the contemplative life consists in raising the mind to the Lord, in an attentive heart, in mental prayer, and, through such exercise, in the contemplation of spiritual things.

A man should not abandon the active life when he has become practiced in it, not even when he has arrived at the contemplative life, for it assists the contemplative life and elevates it.

20. *Answer to a Brother Requesting Instructions on the Eremitic Life.*

We do not flee people who are of the same nature as we and bear the same name of Christ; but we flee the vices they create, as was said to the great Arsenios: "Flee people and save yourself."

21. *Instructions to a Novice*

While doing manual work, or when you are anywhere on a set task, continually repeat this prayer: "Lord Jesus Christ, have mercy upon me, a sinner." During the prayer, attend to yourself, that is, gather up your mind and unite it with your heart. At first, recite it with mental effort, paying attention to each word separately. Later, when the Lord has warmed your heart with the heat of His grace and has united this prayer in you into a single breath, it will flow in you without ceasing, and will always be with you to rejoice and nourish you.

NOTES

INTRODUCTORY

By Constantine Cavarnos

[1] See my book *The Holy Mountain,* Belmont, Mass., 1973, 1977, pp. 43-44.

[2] The appellation "The Virgin of Compassion" denotes an icon of the Theotokos in which she appears with the Child Christ, and is known in Greek as *Eleousa.* Such is the famous icon known as "Our Lady of Vladimir." But from the descriptions we have of the icon possessed by St. Seraphim, the Virgin was shown on it without Christ. In the light of these descriptions, the appellation "The Virgin of Compassion," or "The Virgin of Tenderness," has been improperly applied to the Saint's icon. According to Valentine Zander, the icon which the Saint possessed was of the Theotokos as she appears in the *Annunciation,* with eyes lowered, listening humbly to the words of the Archangel Gabriel, who was not included in this particular icon (*St. Seraphim of Sarov,* New York, 1975, p. 24, n. 1). Another view is that the All-Holy Virgin of his icon was taken from a *Deesis*—an icon in which Christ is shown enthroned, flanked on either side by the Virgin and St. John the Baptist. If this was actually the case, Seraphim was probably inspired to adopt such an icon, to keep an ever-burning sacred lamp before it, and to pray in front of it, by

the example of St. Symeon the New Theologian, who, according to his disciple and biographer Niketas Stethatos, had precisely such an icon in his cell with an everburning lamp before it (*Tou Hosiou Symeon tou Neou Theologou ta Heuriskomena,* "The Extant Works of Saint Symeon the New Theologian," Syros, 1886, Part I, p. 17). St. Seraphim's icon does not survive. There is an icon held by some to be a late version of the icon which the Saint had. There is no certainty about this claim, and in any case even if this icon *is* a version of his icon, we *cannot* assume that it is a replica, for a "version" may be quite other than the original in style, expression and other respects. In making a copy of a traditional icon, a modernist iconographer tends to "perfect" it in the light of modern Western prototypes and techniques.

[3] Regarding this book, see my *Byzantine Thought and Art,* Belmont, Mass., 1968, 1974, pp. 48-58; *St. Macarios of Corinth,* Belmont, 1972, 1977, pp. 23-25, 96-101; and *St. Nicodemos the Hagiorite,* Belmont, 1974, 1979, pp. 14-18, 20-22.

[4] Cf. V. Zander, *op. cit.,* p. 19.

[5] Nikodemos Gkatziroulis, *Ho Serapheim tou Saroph,* "Seraphim of Sarov," 2nd ed., Athens, 1973, p. 27.

[6] V. Zander, *op. cit.,* pp. 47-48.

[7] *Ibid.,* p. 61.

[8] G. P. Fedotov, *A Treasury of Russian Spirituality,* London, 1950, pp. 255, 263.

[9] V. Zander, *op cit.,* p. xvi; cf. Timothy Ware, *The Orthodox Church,* Baltimore, 1964, p. 133.

[10] Franklin Jones, *The Spiritual Instructions of Saint Seraphim of Sarov,* Los Angeles, 1973, p. ix.

[11] G. P. Fedotov, *op. cit.,* p. 245.

[12] Boris Bobrinskoy, in V. Zander, *op. cit.,* p. vii.

[13] *Ibid.,* p. xi.

[14] See my book *The Holy Mountain,* pp. 44-45.

[15] *Ibid.,* pp. 51-53.

[16] *A Treasury of Russian Spirituality,* p. 243. This statement contradicts the one quoted earlier, that St. Seraphim "was the forerunner of the new form of spirituality. . . . "

[17] *Ibid.,* p. 261.

[18] Victor Matthaiou, *Ho Megas Synaxaristes tes Othodoxou Ekklesias* ("The Great Book of Lives of Saints of the Orthodox Church"), Vol. 7, Athens, 1950, p. 71.

[19] *Ibid.,* Vol. 10, 1950, pp. 22-23.

[20] Nicodemos the Hagiorite, *Neon Eklogion* ("New Eklogion," i.e. New Anthology of Lives of Saints), 3rd ed., Athens, 1971, pp. 307-308.

[21] *Ibid.,* p. 310.

[22] *Ibid.,* p. 174.

[23] *The Extant Works,* Part I, p. 17.

[24] *Ibid.,* p. 19.

[25] See *New Eklogion,* p. 315.

[26] *Patrologia Graeca,* Vol. 87³, col. 2921B-C.

[27] Regarding this book, see my *St. Nicodemos the Hagiorite,* pp. 18-22.

[28] *Evergetinos,* Vol. 1, Athens, 1957, p. 79.

[29] *The Extant Works,* Part I, p .6.

[30] Elias Mastrogiannopoulos, *Historia ton Monachon tes Aigyptou* ("History of the Monks of Egypt"), Athens, 1970, pp. 106-107.

[31] *Philokalia,* Vol. 5, Athens, 1963, p. 93.

[32] *The Ladder of Divine Ascent,* New York, n.d. (*ca.* 1960), p. 135.

[33] *Ibid*.

[34] *Philokalia*, Vol. 1, Athens, 1957, p. 256.

[35] *Philokalia*, Vol. 5, p. 92.

[36] *Evergetinos*, Vol. 1, pp. 19-20.

[37] E. Mastrogiannopoulos, *op. cit.*, p. 55.

[38] Nicodemos the Hagiorite, *Biblos Psychophelestate ton en Hagiois Pateron hemon Barsanouphiou kai Ioannou* ("A Most Edifying Book by our Fathers Saints Barsanouphios and John"), Volos, 1960, p. 22.

[39] Sophronios Eustratiadis, *Hagiologion tes Orthodoxou Ekklesias* ("Hagiology of the Orthodox Church"), Athens, 1960, pp. 347-348.

[40] V. Zander, *Saint Seraphim of Sarov*, London, 1968, p. 13.

[41] See my books *St. Macarios of Corinth*, pp. 19-21, and *St. Nicodemos the Hagiorite*, pp. 21-22.

[42] See my *St. Macarios of Corinth*, pp. 15-31.

[43] Vol. 5, pp. 105-106.

[44] Zander, *op. cit.*, p. 44.

THE LIFE OF ST. SERAPHIM

By Mary-Barbara Zeldin

[1] Ivan Kologrivof, *Essai sur la sainteté en Russie*, Bruges, 1953, p. 426.

[2] All dates are given according to the Julian calendar, earlier than the Gregorian, in use in the West, by eleven days in the 18th century, by twelve in the 19th, and by thirteen in the 20th. Thus, July 19, 1759, as given here, is July 30 in the West.

3 Prochoros, the name of the disciple of St. John the Evangelist. He followed St. John into exile in Patmos, where the latter dictated to him the Book of Revelation.

4 The church was dedicated to St. Sergius of Radonezh. It was built in the style of Rostrelli, recently popularized by the building of the Winter Palace in St. Petersburg. In 1833, this church was raised to the status of a cathedral.

5 More exactly, "a fool for Christ's sake" (*yurodivyi*). Such was the name given to those extraordinary individuals who, in order to turn people from materialist interests back to the profundity of the Gospel message, and yet to make evident its accessibility to simple minds as well as to the wise and clever, simulated madness. Such persons are not peculiar to Russia: there were fools for Christ (Gr. *saloi*) in Byzantium as well, notably Symeon (d. *ca.* 550) and Andrew (880-946). The expression goes back to the New Testament (1 Cor. 4: 10) and the tradition of the Hebrew prophets. In Russia, thirty-six such "fools" have been officially recognized as saints. The most famous is St. Basil the Blessed (d. *ca.* 1550), who was officially declared a saint in 1588. St. Basil is buried in Red Square, in Moscow, in the church that popularly bears his name, but is actually dedicated to the Theotokos. "Blessed" was the epithet for such saints, taken from the Beatitude: "Blessed are the poor in spirit." Kologrivof devotes a chapter of his already mentioned book to these "lay saints" (pp. 261-273). See also George Fedotov, *The Russian Religious Mind,* Vol. 2, *The Thirteenth to the Fifteenth Centuries,* ed. with a Foreword by John Meyendorff, Cambridge, Mass., 1966, Ch. XII.

6 Kologrivof, *op. cit.,* p. 419.

7 Literally, a "Starets" is an old man, like the Greek word *Geron.* In monastic usage, a Starets is a Spiritual Father or Guide. Such Elders (*Startsi,* Gr. *Gerontes*) existed in Egypt, in Byzantium, and still exist on Mount Athos. The term came to be applied to monks who directed monastics and laymen through spiritual conversations, counsels and exhortations. In Russia, the *starchestvo,* spiritual guidance, became an institu-

tion re-established by Father Paissy Velichkovsky (1722-1794), who spent seventeen years on Mount Athos. Paissy was imbued with the spirit and practice of silent prayer and inner activity. By his example, his life in monastic administration in Moldavia, and his teaching and writing, he wholly renewed the spirit of Russian monasticism and, through it, much of Russian religious life.

[8] Anonymous writer, *Prepodobny Seraphim Sarovskii: Zhitie. Beceda c Motovilovym,* Paris, 1953, p. 10.

[9] But he evidently did not forget his youthful assistance in the family business, making metaphorical use of its ways when useful in his counseling. See below, "A Conversation with the Saint."

[10] Zander, *St. Seraphim of Sarov,* 1975, p. 5.

[11] On entering monastic life, Ioann received the name of Isaac. On taking the stricter monastic vows, assuming the *Great Schema,* he once again received the name Ioann. The change of names has led to some confusion among historians of the monastery. See V. N. Ilyn, *Prepodobny Seraphim Sarovsky,* 2nd ed., Paris, 1930, pp. 11-12.

[12] The Patriarchate was abolished by Peter the Great in 1721 and replaced by a Synod of bishops. It was re-established in 1918.

[13] During the reign of Catherine II, of some 900 monasteries still in existence more than 60% were closed, and a decree was issued forbidding the founding of new ones without government permission. Since the monasteries even then represented, especially in the more remote districts, the only centers of culture and of charitable work, their closure not only was a spiritual loss, but also resulted in both intellectual decline and physical suffering.

[14] Kologrivof, *op. cit.,* p. 420.

[15] St. Pachomios (286-346) is the founder of Christian

coenobitic monasticism. His rule requires obedience, poverty, chastity, and communal prayer. Communal meals are not required. The requirement of communal meals is one of the modifications made by St. Basil the Great. The rule of St. Pachomios and its modified version by St. Basil require the permission of the Abbot for austerities beyond those commonly practiced at the monastery.

[16] A monumental anthology of writings of Eastern ascetic-mystical Fathers, compiled by St. Macarios of Corinth (1731-1805) and edited by St. Nicodemos the Hagiorite (1749-1809), who also contributed an introduction and brief biographies of the Fathers whose writings are included in it, was published under the title of *Philokalia* at Venice in 1782. They were translated into Slavonic by Paissy Velichkovsky and published in Petersburg in 1793. Much later—between 1876 and 1890—they were translated into Russian by Bishop Theophan the Recluse. They remain the most important guide for Orthodox monks in the way of mystical asceticism. (See Constantin de Grunwald, *Saints of Russia,* trans. by Roger Capel, New York, 1960, p. 163; Constantine Cavarnos, *Byzantine Thought and Art,* Belmont, Mass., 1968, 1974, pp. 48-58.) Although these writings were thus not available in print at the time of St. Seraphim's novitiate, the monks made handwritten copies of texts by the ascetic-mystical Fathers.

[17] St. Dmitri of Rostov gave the title of *Menaion* to his collection of the lives of the saints and commentaries on their feasts, arranged as in the *Menaia* proper. The *Menaia* are twelve volumes, one for each month, containing the services for the saints for each day.

[18] It might be observed that at the age of thirty-five St. Seraphim left the coenobitic life for that of a hermit.

[19] For further instructions to novices see Counsel 21.

[20] In Hebrew "seraphic" means fiery or ardent.

[21] Disapproval of the type of spiritual fervor and outlook characteristic of St. Seraphim was not uncommon in Russian

monasteries. The Startsi of Optino met with the same attitude. See, e.g., de Grunwald, *op. cit.,* p. 165.

[22] An hieromonk (Gr. *hieromonachos*) is a monk who is also a priest.

[23] Gr. *Mesonyktikon.*

[24] These are Psalms used as the continuation or conclusion of the Hours.

[25] Compline.

[26] Anonymous, *Prepodobny Seraphim Sarovsky,* p. 18.

[27] *Aegopodium podagria* Linnaeus, commonly called goutweed, ashweed, or ground elder in English. The plant is native to the greater part of temperate Europe, European and Asiatic Russia, and Japan. It is related to celery, parsnip, carrot, angelica, cumin, etc., looks like parsnip as to leaves but has yellow flowers. In Medieval times it was used as a palliative for gout and was eaten then and later as a salad or boiled vegetable. "Ground elder makes spicy and tolerable eating if the leaves are boiled like spinach" (G. Grigson, *The Englishman's Flora,* London, 1955, p. 112).

[28] This gives support to the suggestion that Alexander I did not die in 1825 in Taganrog but, following the counsel of the Starets, left his royal surroundings to become a monk, later identified as Starets Kuzmich, who lived to a very old age in Siberia. The story was popular and became widespread. In the twenties of the present century, the Soviet Government had Alexander I's coffin opened. It was found to contain nothing but stones. (The coffin had also been opened in the first decade of this century. No remains were found at that time either. The event was not publicized.)

[29] Kologrivof, *op, cit.,* p. 426.

[30] The Metropolitan of Moscow was the titular head of the Monastery of the Holy Trinity-St. Sergius, which was founded in the first half of the 14th century by St. Sergius of Radonezh

(the former name of Zagorsk). After the Monastery of Kiev-Pechersky, which officially outranked it, the Monastery of the Holy Trinity-St. Sergius was the most important in Russia until the Revolution of 1917. It is known for providing the moral force which united the Russians against invaders, notably against the Mongols in 1380—during St. Sergius' lifetime—and again in the first part of the 17th century, during the "Time of Troubles." In 1748, it was granted an orphanage and a seminary. The latter became the most famous of the religious academies in Russia, and a center of religious studies and of spirituality, especially under Philaret who, as Metropolitan of Moscow, was its head from 1821 to 1867.

31 The expression is Zander's *op. cit.,* p. 63.

32 See "A Conversation with the Saint," by Nicholas A. Motovilov," in the present book.

33 In 1862, after a long investigation and through the help of the community's foster father, Nicholas Motovilov, and of St. Seraphim's old friend Father Antony (whom the Saint had asked not to forget his "orphant girls" and who, now Abbot at Zagorsk, was able to intercede directly with Metropolitan Philaret), Diveyevo was officially raised to the rank of a convent, that of "Seraphim-Diveyevo," and placed under the jurisdiction of the Bishop of Tambov. For further details of the difficulties encountered by the community and the history of Diveyevo after the repose of St. Seraphim, see e.g. Zander, *op. cit.,* pp. 64-70, and Ch. 9 *passim.*

A CONVERSATION WITH THE SAINT

TRANSLATED BY MARY-BARBARA ZELDIN

1 Nicholas Alexandrovich Motovilov wrote this account in his memoirs, probably only a short time after the event itself, which took place in November, 1831. After Motovilov's death in 1879, it remained at Diveyevo in the keeping of his widow, Yelena, who had been brought up there and who returned there to live when her husband died. Shortly before her own death, Yelena Motovilova handed it, along with the rest of her

husband's papers, to the writer Serge Nilus. The papers were
in total disorder, covered with dust and feathers and droppings
of birds who had nested in the attic, where the archives had
been lodged. With remarkable patience and persistence, Nilus
sorted them out and managed—miraculously, he himself sug-
gests—to decipher Motovilov's almost illegible handwriting.
About a year later, in May 1903, Nilus published the Conversation in the *Moscow Gazette.*

[2] St. Seraphim's Scriptural quotations are almost always ac-
curate according to the Bible in Slavonic. Sometimes, two
words are transposed. I have given the Bagster English translation and reference in the case of the Old Testament passages and the King James version in the case of the New
Testament ones, except for occasional changes which I have
made in order to bring the translation closer the precise meaning of the Greek text. Wherever there was greater divergence
from the Slavonic, I have given the reference to the passage
St. Seraphim seems obviously to have in mind.

[3] *Bogolyubye.* Compare the Greek, *Philotheos,* "God-loving
one."

[4] The Russian term *dobrodyetel,* used here and frequently
later on in the Conversation, has the double meaning of
"good works" and "virtue." I am translating it either way, according to its appropriate sense in the context.

[5] Part of a morning prayer.

[6] *Bogu lyubezny.* See Note 3, above.

[7] See prayer and anointing with Holy Chrism in the Office
of Chrismation.

[8] *Sladost.* The Russian word, literally "sweetness," also re-
tains figuratively its original Slavonic meaning of "pleasure"
and "delight." Since the concern here is in good part with
Motovilov's experiences in terms of the five senses, "sweetness" is a better rendering, although it does not fit so well with
the subsequent quotation from Psalm 35:9, where the same
word is used in Slavonic and hence translates as "pleasure."

SPIRITUAL COUNSELS OF THE SAINT

TRANSLATED BY MARY-BARBARA ZELDIN

[1] The *Spiritual Counsels* of St. Seraphim were never printed in their original form. Written down in 1839—six years after the repose of the Saint—by Hieromonk Serge, they were revised by Metropolitan Philaret, "partly in order to put them into proper grammatical form, partly so that thoughts which were not expressed sufficiently fully or were expressed in an unusual manner should not be misinterpreted." (Letter of Metropolitan Philaret to Archimandrite Antony, Abbot of the Monastery of the Holy Trinity-Saint Sergius, as published in Russian in V. N. Ilyin, *Prepodobny Seraphim Sarovsky,* 2nd rev. ed., Paris, 1930, pp. 152-153.) The revised *Spiritual Counsels* were finally approved by the Holy Synod and first published in 1841 as appendices to Father Serge's *Short Sketch of the Life of Starets Mark, Monk and Hermit of the Monastery of Sarov.* There they number thirty-three. Later collections include additional counsels. I have selected twenty-one counsels as they appear in Leonid Denisov's *Zhitie prepodobnavo ottsa nashevo Seraphima Sarovskavo,* Moscow, 1904, pp. 420-463, and present them here in somewhat abridged form. Denisov's collection includes some additions to the original thirty-three and some variants of these.

[2] Paraphrased from the *Philokalia,* "On Silence."

SELECTED BIBLIOGRAPHY

Anonymous, *Prepodobny Seraphim Sarovsky*: *Zhi-tie; Beceda c Motovilovym* ("Saint Seraphim of Sarov: Life; Conversation with Motovilov"). Paris, 1953.

Anonymous, *A Conversation of Saint Seraphim of Sarov with N. A. Motovilov*: *A Wonderful Revelation to the World*. Jordanville, N. Y., 1962.

Arseniev, Nicholas, *Russian Piety*. 2nd ed. Trans. by A. Moorhouse. Crestwood, N. Y., 1975.

Cavarnos, Constantine, *The Holy Mountain*. Belmont, Massachusetts, 1973, 1977.

Fedotov, G. P., *The Russian Religious Mind,* Vol. 1, *Kievan Christianity*: *The Tenth to the Thirteenth Centuries,* Cambridge, Mass., 1946; Vol. 2, *The Middle Ages*: *The Thirteenth and Fifteenth Centuries,* ed. with a Foreword by John Meyendorff, Cambridge, Mass., 1966.

Fedotov, G. P., *A Treasury of Russian Spirituality*. London, 1950.

Gatziroulis, Nikodemos, *Ho Serapheim tou Saroph* ("Seraphim of Sarov"). Athens, 1966. 2nd ed. 1973.

Gorainoff, Irina, *Seraphim de Sarov: Sa vie; Entretien avec Motovilov et Instructions spirituelles* ("Seraphim of Sarov: His Life; and Conversation with Motovilov and Spiritual Instructions"), trans. from the Russian by I. Gorainoff. Bégrolles en Mauges, Maine et Loire: Abbaye de la Bellefontaine, Collection Spiritualité orientale, No. 11, 1973.

Gorodetzky, Nadejda, *The Humiliated Christ in Modern Russian Thought*. London and New York, 1938.

Grunwald, Constantin de, *Saints of Russia*. Trans. by Roger Capel. New York, 1960.

Ilyin, V. N., *Prepodobny Seraphim Sarovsky*, ("Saint Seraphim of Sarov"). 2nd, rev. ed. Paris, 1930.

Kologrivof, Ivan, *Essai sur la sainteté en Russie* ("Essay on Saintliness in Russia"). Bruges, 1953.

Kontoglou, Photios, *Serapheim tou Saroph, ho Polyagapemenos Hagios* ("Seraphim of Sarov, the Much-loved Saint"), *Eleutheria* (Athens), Nov. 11, 18, 25, Dec. 2, 1962. Trans. by Constantine Cavarnos. Manuscript.

Mastrogiannopoulos, Elias, *Historia ton Monachon tes Aigyptou* ("History of the Monks of Egypt"). Athens, 1970.

Meyendorff, John, *Byzantine Theology: Historical Trends and Doctrinal Themes.* 2nd ed. New York, 1976.

Meyendorff, John, *A Study of Gregory Palamas.* Trans. by George Lawrence. London, 1964.

Nicodemos the Hagiorite, St., *Neon Eklogion* ("New Collection of Lives of Saints"). 3rd ed., Athens, 1974.

Pascal, Pierre, *Civilisation paysanne en Russie,* Vol. 2, *La Religion du peuple russe* ("Peasant Civilization in Russia," Vol. 2, "The Religion of the Russian People"). Lausanne, 1973.

Putyatin, A., "Zhizn Svyatovo Prepodobnovo Seraphim Sarovskovo" ("The Life of the Blessed Saint Seraphim of Sarov"), *Yedynaya Tserkov: One Church,* 7 (June, 1953), 10-13.

Putyatin, A., "Zhitie i Proslavlenye Prepodobnovo Seraphima, Sarovskovo Chudotvortsa" ("Life and Glorification of Saint Seraphim of Sarov, the Miracle Worker") , conclusion of the above article, *Ibid.* (no number or date, but probably July, 1953) , 5-8.

Ware, Timothy, *The Orthodox Church,* Baltimore, 1963.

Zander, Valentine, *Saint Seraphim of Sarov: His Life.* Trans. from the French edition of 1953. London, 1968.

Zander, Valentine, *St. Seraphim of Sarov.* Trans. by Sister Gabriel Anne. Introduction by Boris Bobrinskoy. New York, 1975.

INDEX

INDEX